The Forsaken Lover

The
Forsaken
Lover

*White words and
black people*

Chris Searle

Routledge & Kegan Paul
London and Boston

First published 1972
by Routledge & Kegan Paul Ltd
Broadway House, 68–74 Carter Lane,
London EC4V 5EL and
9 Park Street,
Boston, Mass. 02108, U.S.A.
Printed in Great Britain by
Western Printing Services Ltd
Bristol

ISBN 0 7100 7283 X

To the Children of Tobago,
who began my education.

Contents

Acknowledgments

The author and publishers wish to thank the following for permission to reproduce the works cited, or extracts from them:

Extracts from *Rights of Passage* and *Islands* by Edward Brathwaite, both published by Oxford University Press.
Jonathan Cape Ltd for extract from 'Laventille', *The Castaway*, by Derek Walcott.
Farrar, Straus & Giroux Inc. for extract from *The Gulf* by Derek Walcott, copyright © 1963, 1964, 1965, 1969, 1970 by Derek Walcott.
Basil Smith for *The Church*.
Marguerite Wyke for *History Leaves No Memorials to the Poor*.

All possible care has been taken to trace ownership of extracts included in the volume and to make full acknowledgment of their use.

Introduction

My first impulse is to question my authority in writing and compiling this book. I am dealing with perhaps the most sprawling and amorphous of concepts, and I am writing about children who wear a different skin to mine and experience a completely different society and environment. I am a white middle-class Englishman from the London suburbs discussing the education of black children in a Caribbean island. The situation is absurd enough to begin with, even though I spent a year among them as an English teacher in a secondary school in Tobago. A knowledge of one's own identity is something each individual spends a lifetime in chasing in the context of his fellows. I can only say that from what I have seen and read, the West Indian probably has a greater problem of identity than most other people. In Tobago and the Windward Islands he is predominantly ex-African, his ancestors shoved on to a Caribbean island by white pirates perhaps three centuries ago; he is displaced to an extent that only he knows:[1]

> We left
> somewhere a life we never found,
>
> customs and gods that are not born again,
> some crib, some grill of light
> clanged shut on us in bondage, and withheld
>
> us from that world below us and beyond,
> and in its swaddling cerements we're still bound.

My first slim experience teaching West Indian children in England suggests to me that the statements made in this work on language and alienation apply to them perhaps with even greater force. They have moved towards a further degree of displacement. As English people they may find a new identity. As English people with black skins speaking English in England, they have a new identity which may speak against them if their teachers are not wary.

It is with these thoughts and cautions that I write this account, more as editor and commentator than critic, with the feeling that at as many times as possible, words of West Indian, child and man, shall speak out for themselves. Their experience is far more valid than any objective notion that I can claim to make: 'I have not wished to be objective. Besides, that would be dishonest. It is not possible for me to be objective . . . Why not quite the simple attempt to touch the other, to feel the other, to explain the other to myself?'[2]

As new nations emerge, and struggle against a colonial legacy and previous structures of domination, the issue of 'Identity' becomes a conscious and anxious preoccupation for their peoples. 'Who am I?' 'What is this place?' 'Who are these people around me?' 'Do I belong to these people?' These are all questions that loom suddenly out of the phlegmatic acceptance of the old order. A notion of identity involves the connexion and sympathy a man feels with himself, and the people and places around him that are built into his world, with a feeling of belongingness in that world, that a man's special uniqueness has a definite place there.

A culture, said E. H. Erikson, must 'provide an early basis' for the identity of a child. He needs to feel, as he grows towards adolescence, that there is a structure of 'meaningful wider belongingness'[3] behind his relationship with himself and his family, some supporting social strength in which he can trust. In addition to this fundamental need, the West Indian child has to integrate his own life-cycle within the upheaval of the changing state of his country's political identity as it becomes a disparate political entity—an island nation. He may be a West Indian abroad, but at home he is a Trinidadian, a Grenadian, a St Lucian. Even in an uneasy unity between two islands like Trinidad and Tobago, a Trinidadian is still a Trinidadian and a Tobagonian still a Tobagonian. But as these new, separate nations find their independent political identities, their people still speak in a language that takes them back to the past and their subjection and exploitation through centuries of slavery and colonialism. They also inevitably retain many of the old forms: their skins tell of Africa and Asia, their religions of Canterbury and Rome, the political institutions of Europe and America. Their economies draw from New York, Canada and London, and their education system speaks of Oxford and Cambridge Examining Boards. And they live on islands, some only a few miles from the South American coast. Their language speaks against them and tells them that 'black' is a bad word, a word of guilt and doubt and evil, but that 'white' has its associations with purity, goodness and innocence. Their old identity was one of imitation, subservience and alienation, cutting them off from themselves and their own dignity. Their new identity must speak of them and their own world, for their own ideas and standards, their language and their art.

We find our identities through our language. That language must uphold us, give us confidence, tell us we belong to our world and each other. If our world is an island, it must make our island ours, not dissipate it to an alien mass and leave us a void. It is our language that provides us with the particular dominant national images that sustain our particular culture, and build the structure of belongingness and trust that most people need, giving to the individual self the ability to experience the necessary social sense of continuity and sameness. A man becomes absurd when his language divides him from his world, divorces him from his surroundings and his fellows, and makes him speak of foreign things. It is his language that forges out and articulates his images of identity: 'One uses the language which helps to preserve one's life, which helps to make one feel at peace with the world, and which screens out the greatest amount of chaos.'[4]

But in the European language of the Caribbean black man there is disorder and chaos. It is the disorder of mimicry. The language tenses with the nature. The words and images mock the man who speaks and feels them. He covers himself with foreignness. 'Nothing is more astonishing than to hear a black man express himself properly, for then in truth he is putting on a white world . . . he is a complete replica of the white man. So there is nothing to do but give in.'[5]

1

Monostatus

The reader of this work is urged to read the testament of Frantz Fanon in his *Black Skin White Masks*. It is the most powerful statement on the Caribbean black man's problem of identity and struggles with the white world that I have read. While I was reading it, I found myself saying, 'I must quote all this book. This man has felt and known and *is* everything I have to say. It is all inside him.' From his book, Fanon heaves himself and his blackness at the reader, giving him another, separate existence. I found myself turning to his work after I had written my own account, and his words and insights seemed to be what I had been struggling to find by being amongst others with a different coloured skin from mine. What I have to say comes from outside a black skin, based on my experience with others. Fanon speaks from inside blackness, based on his experience as himself. His statements crystallize, from a man's own existence on another island, what I have to say from my own:[1]

> We understand now why the black man cannot take pleasure in his insularity. For him there is only one way out, and it leads into the white world.
>
> Every colonized people—in other words, every people in whose soul an inferiority complex has been created by the death and burial of its local cultural originality—finds itself face to face with the language of the civilizing nation, that is, with the culture of the mother country.
>
> Willy-nilly, the [Caribbean] Negro has to wear the livery that the white world has sewed for him.

4

White civilization and European culture have forced an existential deviation on the Negro.

Imprisoned on his island, lost in the atmosphere that offers not the slightest outlet, the Negro breathes in the appeal of Europe like pure air.

The same day that I was reading *Black Skin White Masks*, I went in the evening to see *The Magic Flute* by Mozart. I knew very little about the opera, and nothing about the story. I think that I was still thinking about Fanon. Then the overture and the first scene: the flowing beauty, the order of the sounds—the artifice of genius. 'But what is this now? A black man on the stage? What is he doing here?' Ah, 'Monostatus, a negro in the service of Sarastro.' But look how he moves like a clown. Look how the white man who plays him gives him all his ridicule. Look how he makes his eyes roll. Look how he ogles the white, pure heroine and now tries to rape her. Look how the fool in feathers calls him the devil. Look how he is pulled off the stage to be whipped by some white men. Look how he grovels at the feet of his white master, the epitome of wisdom, enlightenment and truth. Listen how his master tells him, 'Your soul is as black as your face.' Look how he falls down into darkness and punishment like the other evil characters at the end of the play. All in Mozart, all within the forms and moulds of art and beauty, all inside the same time and same day as Fanon's open soul.

Then there *is* more to be said. The thing must be said again, and again. We take school parties of our children to see *The Magic Flute*, and Fanon is still almost an unknown name, just a vague scare of blackness. We laugh at the grotesque Monostatus, the black bogey man, and applaud the white world of art that his distorted shape fits into. It still suits us to remember him that way. We do not want to know the black man. We do not want to climb inside him. We would rather have our fools and caricatures and hoist them in the name of beauty, tradition and myth. We turn our back on real men, real existence, real blackness. We do not want to read and experience Fanon:[2]

I cannot go to a film without seeing myself. I wait for me. In the interval, just before the film starts, I wait for me.

The people in the theatre are watching me, examining me, waiting for me. A Negro groom is going to appear. My heart makes my head swim.

But what to do with Monostatus? He is a legend and a funny black sheep that we and our children accept and laugh at, and soon enough we extend feelings for the myth to cover the reality. Then what do we say to ourselves and our children? That he isn't really as foolish as Monostatus? That it was the ignorance of the Age of Reason that has been passed down to us and perpetuates itself in us? What if the children we tell are black themselves? How do we explain this sudden distortion of their own existence?

The Little Black Boy

My mother bore me in the southern wild,
And I am black, but O! my soul is white;
White as an angel is the English child,
But I am black, as if bereav'd of light.

My mother taught me underneath a tree,
And sitting down before the heat of day,
She took me on her lap and kissed me,
And pointing to the east, began to say:

'Look on the rising sun: there God does live,
And gives his light, and gives his heat away;
And flowers and trees and beasts and men receive
Comfort in morning, joy in the noonday

And we are put on earth a little space,
That we may learn to bear the beams of love:
And these black bodies and this sunburnt face
Is but a cloud, and like a shady grove.

For when our souls have learn'd the heat to bear,
The cloud will vanish: we shall hear his voice,
Saying: "Come out of the grove, my love and care,
And round my golden tent like lambs rejoice".'

Thus did my mother say, and kissed me;

And thus I say to little English boy.
When I from black and he from white cloud free,
And round the tent of God like lambs we joy,

I'll shade him from the heat, till he can bear
To lean in joy upon our father's knee;
And then I'll stand and stroke his silver hair,
And be like him, and he will then love me.

William Blake, another eighteenth-century white man, in a 'song of innocence' gives a statement of blackness. The black boy feels guilty about his blackness. He can only see himself in relation to the white world, and the white 'angelic' child. So he must convince the world that, despite the blackness of his skin, his soul is white and pure. The eternal part of him must be white, he says. His blackness is only a cover, only a cloud to evaporate when he dies, to reveal his beautiful white soul beneath. Christian symbolism has always venerated whiteness: the dove, the lamb, the robe, the white brightness of purity and holiness. 'God is light', only the evil is dark. Christianity, essentially and historically a white man's religion, is built on the vindication of whiteness and white symbols. Consequently it has been used as an emotive weapon to enslave and degrade the black man. English children still write in each others' autograph books:

> God made the little black boys
> He made them in the night
> He made them in a hurry
> And forgot to paint them white.

The Church was very effective in the vanguard of colonialism: no black Christian proselyte wanted a black soul. Christianity seemed to give the possibility of becoming white, eternally white: in the next world. It offered black skins, white souls. Blake's poem is a symptom of the insidiousness of the white man's symbolism, built as it is on the positivism of white and the negativism of black, the rightness and dignity of white and the wrongness and degradation of black. The white God gives his light to the black man, bestowing his power in the name of

truth. The sun rises in the east, but for the black mother and child it rises over Europe:

> Look on the rising sun: there God does live,
> And gives his light, and gives his heat away . . .

The white heat of power and subjection is accepted by the mother as beams of love from the white God. These must be endured. The black mother urges acceptance, stoicism to her son: their blackness will eventually and providentially pass away, and they will step out good and white from their shady grove in the southern wild, to play with the white children and stroke their silver, flowing hair. Then the white children will love the little black boy. As long as he becomes white in mind and belief, throws off his blackness and worships at the white altar, shades the white boy from the sun and idolizes his hair texture, he will be accepted by the white boy. But only as long as he promises to be white:

> And be like him, and he will then love me.

Until he becomes white he is unacceptable, even in the eyes of the white man's God. He will only find acceptance as idolater of the white boy's whiteness, saving him from the heat, envying his white beauty with fondling and stroking of the white boy's hair. To the white world, the black boy can only find his identity in terms of submission and service to the white way of life. This is the identity that the black boy learns through the white man's language, schools and churches, and it is an identity that embitters and alienates him.

The little black boy is different now. He has a new view of his mother, his history and himself. He sees the domination of white and the role of the white man's church in keeping him unaware of the rightness of his blackness. In 1970 he is very angry about these things:[3]

The Church

It was here
by the wall of the

little white church
a young black mother,
her belly big
with child and
future generations,
was eaten down
to pulp
by the chattering
shells of a Thompson automatic.
Their pure, red blood
soaked the building
to its festering foundations.

More,
many more of us
died
within the walls
of this gateway to deliverance
which stands at the heart
of our village,
the sum total of Europe's generosity.
The soil on which
it sits
being but dust in the eye
of her greed.

Now,
We wrap the bodies in
the music of goat-skins
and lift our voices
to a God so fearsome,
He has but one cheek.

                                        Basil Smith

Blake's 1789 'Song of Innocence' was a poem about how a black mother educated her child. The mother's voice of experience urged stoicism to the child: accept the life on earth, and the slave identity which comes with it. In 1971 there is *Soledad Brother*, also about education. George Jackson educated himself from his own experience, the journey of his own consciousness as he became more and more aware of his wounded identity as a black man in a white world. His education in prison involved the unlearning of the white man's view of the black man, pushed into him by his formal schooling and his mother's protectiveness. In prison his education was a war with himself and his own identity as a black American: 'the greatest battle is with oneself'. Like Blake's black child, Jackson had his first education from his mother: the education for acceptance and survival. From prison he wrote to his mother that 'experience has made me better informed', and his real education through experience and awareness forms a gradual rejection of his mother's advice:[4]

> If I followed the advice I receive it would only serve to enslave me further to this madness of our times . . .

> I feel that you have failed me, Mama. I know that you have failed me.

The little Black Boy did not turn round to his mother and answer

> I've been alone for a long time. This is why I've had so much pain and trouble . . . You gave me god and that horrible church. Even god managed to take something away from me. I have nothing left but myself.

Soledad Brother is a poem of experience. It is what the child shouts back at the mother when he begins to know his world:

> Why did you allow us to worship at a white altar? Why even now, following tragedy after tragedy, crisis after crisis, do you still send Jon to that school where he is taught to feel inferior, and why do you continue to send me Easter cards? This is the height of disrespect you show me. You never wanted me to be a man nor Jon neither. You don't want us to defeat our enemies. What is wrong with you, Mama? No other mama in History has acted the way you act under stress situations.
> I won't be a good *boy* ever.

The dancing lamb is the fighting panther, the white idolater becomes the white destroyer. There is no delight for the black boy in enjoying the white life as a subjected, fawning companion of the white child. Blake's black child was an alienated child. His skin is black, but his eyes and mind are set on white. He looks towards the white world and white children and only sees himself imperfect, incomplete, 'bereav'd'. Jackson's eyes were on himself, his black brothers, his freedom. The white world only left him 'alienated and isolated'.

Now these four statements come from black children in England trapped in a white situation, surrounded by white groups. Like Jackson, they all express alienation and isolation:

> There all alone
> isolated and contaminated
> where no-one speaks
> nor hears what you say
> They talk about how
> you dress and how
> you speak
> if I ever speak.
> No one to talk to
> No one no one

> One day a stranger
> knocked on the door
> I opened the door
> for loneliness had gone
> but then the bills man
> enters in with a scorn
> on his face and full of sin.
> Out on the street again
> was met with loneliness
> again with no one
> No one

Walking about the street with my hands in pocket, nobody really cares about me. My only true friend is the black suit I always wear, which I've had for years. People walk about in groups, all gay and laughing, while me, I walk all alone in my old black suit. Suddenly I see someone coming to me, a bunch of boys and girls. How happy I felt. Then it all disappeared again and left me lonely.

> I am very lonely Nowhere to go
> Nowhere to play, not a friend
> To share my grief only myself.
>
> When the sun shines I go outside
> and play with my shadow
> But yet it cannot do me much
> as if I had a friend.
>
> Sometimes when I am dreaming I dream
> of how I play with a lot of girls
> But just as I get up it all go away
>
> Sometimes I say to myself I wish I could
> sleep and dream of friends
> and that my dreams will never
> ends

I dreamed that I was riding on a bicycle and I was going to crash into a wall and the brakes would not work. Then something hooked me and I was stuck in the air. I looked to see who hooked me. I saw nothing. I unhooked myself and went inside a house to see who hooked me. It was a fairly big house, and I looked in all the rooms. I saw a big cupboard that had been left by the owners. I opened it and there were two boys. I said, 'I will not hurt you.' They rushed past me and ran as fast as they could. I never saw them again.

Many children feel alone in claustrophobic city surroundings, the environment of these particular children. But there is a haunting consistency in these statements, the loneliness of the children somehow has a similar pitch throughout. One waits inside her house, 'isolated and contaminated', one wanders down the street with her old black suit which she always wears, one plays with her shadow, another walks through an empty house. They are all forsaken. In each case other children seem to be coming to relieve the loneliness, as if the child has expectations

of comfort and company, but they always fade away, sometimes sharply, sometimes slowly. And there is the sense that
the black child himself accepts the guilt for the disappearance.
White children too can sense this aloneness and forsakenness of
the black child in the white world:

> The little girl stood alone
> I wondered why?
> The white kids called her names
> I wondered why?
> Then I realised . . . she was a coloured child
>
> She looked the same to me
> It seemed all wrong
> She even talked in a London way
> It was all wrong
> But then . . . she was a coloured child

And:

> Alone he walks
> He walks alone
> He has no friends
> And has no home
> I noticed something from the back
> He is alone because he's black.

Or:

> *The Immigrant*
>
> He walks down the lonely street
> With a pair of old shoes on his feet.
> A job he cannot find,
> People say they're a different kind.
>
> They look and point in the street
> And they talk about the things they eat.
> They come to England to make a career
> But people just stop and sneer.
>
> Why? He's your brother
> You should treat him like you
> Treat your mother.

Or there is the feeling that the white children will speak and play only out of conscience or patronage:

> I live in a block of flats where people
> do play I have no friends day after day
> if I have no friend I can't play
> so I stay in and look after myself

> I noticed they started to talk to
> Me it was because I was black
> and they were just saying to theirselves, let's speak
> Don't be rotten

These children speak of the same terrifying alienation and self-condemnation that the little Black Boy was told by his mother to accept, and which George Jackson rejected and fought up to the last moment of his life, loving his blackness:

> I think only of how I live, how well, how nobly. We think
> if we are to be men again we must stop working for
> nothing, competing against each other for the little they
> allow us to possess, stop selling our women or allowing
> them to be used and handled against their will, stop
> letting our children be educated by the barbarian, using
> their language, dress and customs, and most assuredly
> stop turning our cheeks.

The 'innocence' of Blake's little Black Boy is the mystified innocence of black children in England, America, the Caribbean, or in any land where the English have ruled and the English language is spoken by black people. But the lost blackness, the lost identity is being looked for again and being found. Black children, whether they are in a neo-colonial situation like Trinidad and Tobago, or an immigrant situation like England, now have the power and the growing awareness to be conscious of their loss. They are beginning to go on a journey to recover it, like a child who has lost the most treasured part of himself:

> On Friday 9.30 a.m.
> I heard a kitten cry

I went looking for it.
It was in a tree across a river
I wondered how it got there.
So I swam across
but it was no good
the current was drawing me away
I wish I was in a boat
Then I was shouting for help
no one heard me
I was just going over then I fainted
when I woke up the dock attendant said
'I saved your life'
so I thanked him and said,
'I have to be on my way
I am going to save a kitten.'
'Where is it?
What colour is it?'
'It is black,' I said.
'You nearly died for that kitten.'
Then he said,
'It was my kitten it always goes up there.'
So then he sat down and cried.
I said
'Don't cry.'

Our children and ourselves must break the old mythology. As the black man smashes the icons of Monostatus and the little Black Boy, he is destroying parts of our own ignorance, and we must be with him, not against him. Our friendships and our children are more important than the caricatures and myths that we set up about others for the sake of our own pride and power. Fanon only asks for something that we all hope: 'that the tool never possess the man. That the enslavement of man by man cease forever . . . That it may be possible for me to discover and love man, wherever he may be.'[5]

2

The island theme

On the bank of this brook, I found many pleasant
savana's or meadows, plain, smooth and cover'd with
grass; and on the rising parts of them next to the higher
grounds, where the water, as it might be supposed, never
overflow'd, I found a great deal of tobacco, green, and
growing to a great and very strong stalk . . . I came to an
opening, where the country seem'd to descend to the
west, and a little spring of fresh water, which issued
out of the side of the hill by me, run the other way, that
is, due east; and the country appear'd so fresh, so green,
so flourishing, everything being in a constant verdure or
flourish of spring, that it looked like a planted garden.
I descended a little on the side of that delicious vale,
surveying it with a secret kind of pleasure (tho' mixt
with other afflicting thoughts) to think that this was all
my own, that I was king and lord of all this country
indefeasibly, and had a right of possession; and if I could
convey it, I might have it in inheritance as compleatly
as any lord of a manor in England. I saw here abundance
of cocoa trees, orange and lemon, and citron trees; but
all wild and very few bearing any fruit, at least not then.
However, the green limes that I gathered were not only
pleasant to eat, but very wholesome; and I mix'd their
juice afterwards with water, which made it very wholesome, and very cool and refreshing.

Defoe: *Robinson Crusoe*

Advantages of living on an island are, in an island their
will not be much violence, discrimination as in the

countries. In an island the people there will have to
work hard at their jobs whether it is working in a garden
or in a store.

Most of the people there will be hard working people
and when they work for a few cents, all will spend to
feed and clothe a family. Rich people will not mistreat
their servants. If someone is working for some one they
will be treated kindly.

In an island there will be peace and hardly any noise.
The most noise you may here is from the animals playing
in bushes. There will not be many kidnapping many road
deaths and sad scenes.

Children who live on an island will be healthy, cheerful
children, they will be contented and grow up obedient
and hard working in both work and schooling.

On some island there will be lovely beaches with palm
trees and coconut trees. Most of the trees and shrubs
will be there and an artist could make a good scenery
there. Tourism will go on on an island because there will
be quietness, and peace and thats what tourist likes. They
also come to see the beautiful flowers in bloom.

People will be welcome with hospitality on an island more
than in a city. There will be pleasant smiles and friendly
and cheerful greetings as they pass you. They won't be
much haughtiness and quarels about who has more
money . . .

Thirteen-year-old girl

The colonizer and the decolonized, Crusoe and the child of
Friday, are talking about their island. One asserts possession,
the other simply accepts that her island is hers. One sees
produce, fertility and merchandise around him, the other sees
her home and identity, but they both realize that their lives are
concerned with this island, that they have a link, a relationship
with its oneness and its beauty.

English language and poetry have always valued the idea
and image of the Island. It has suggested many themes: man's
own isolation, a dream of beauty, a stage to be passed on a
journey of life, the sanctuary and retreat, the place of escape.
And the world has been an island and the island has been

a Paradise—the themes have often been associated with each
other. The European mind has often had a strange compulsion
to crystallize its myths and dreams in terms of an island, in order
to focus them clearly in a distinct and discrete vision. Shakespeare made his 'Theatrum Mundi', his stage of the world, an
enchanted island where Caliban scraped in the earth. Crusoe
trapped on his island, surrounded by the apparent conditions
of Paradise, worked it into profits. In this century Golding has
played out his history of the world on an island, and Huxley
ended his vision on one, seeing it snatched away by the powers
of commerce and greed. A sixteen-year-old girl writing in an
English school sees an island as a mirage:[1]

> Bewildered in a wilderness I turned
> tormented by the yellow glare of the sun's despair,
> To where a long-sought island stood out clear
> but turned to dust and air as I drew near.

There has been this reoccurring hope of release to an island,
a different, mythical world that the imagination hoists as its
ideal. There is Shelley's island; the image of human perfectibi-
lity:[2]

> Other flowering isles must be
> In the sea of Life and Agony:
> Other spirits float and flee
> O'er that gulf: even now, perhaps,
> On some rock the wild wind wraps,
> With folded wings they waiting sit
> For my back, to pilot it
> To some calm and blooming cove,
> Where for me, and those I love,
> May a windless bower be built,
> Far from passion, pain and guilt,
> In a dell mid lawny hills,
> Which the wild sea-murmur fills,
> And soft sunshine, and the sound
> Of old forests echoing round,
> And the light and smell divine
> Of all flowers that breathe and shine:
> We may live so happy there,

That the spirits of the air,
Envying us, may even entice
To our healing Paradise
The polluting multitude.
. . . And the love which heals all strife
Circling, like the breath of life,
All things in that sweet abode
With its own mild brotherhood:
They, not it, would change; and soon
Every sprite beneath the moon
Would repent its envy vain
And the earth grow young again.

But the transcendent vision of the early nineteenth century becomes the tourist seduction-piece of the twentieth. The vision becomes real, they say, in 'Tranquil Tobago—Crusoe's Island', the two-week, air-conditioned, all-in Eden, the island of the rum-punch and the Bird of Paradise:[3]

Here is a gem. The finest beaches imaginable, and all facilities for water-sports. Enchanting, unspoiled scenery. Tennis, golf. First-class hotels. This island just takes the Caribbean Oscar from Grenada by a short head. For those who do not expect deck-chairs on the beach, a continual whirl of night-life and fabulous shopping, then Tobago is incomparable . . . our first impression was 'here at last is a paradise'.

But these are white men's voices. 'To each his own', the calypsonian announces. An island becomes enough of a world for those people who permanently live on it: 'Grenada for Grenadians, Barbados for Barbadians, Jamaica for Jamaicans', and if Tobago has its own paradise, it will be enough for Tobagonians, as well as for those with dollars enough to come there as tourists:[4]

Your native friend will surely be your host
And show you some of the beauty from coast to coast,
Lovely hotels, lovely beaches, lovely flowers, pretty faces,

> It is grand
> On this Crusoe-land.
> Come le'we go Tobago.
> That Paradise found by Robinson Crusoe . . .
> Now the whol' world say
> Come to Tobago for holiday.

The children of these islands often write of Paradise. They are surrounded and conditioned by the images of both its reality and exploitation. They have so often had the idea heaved upon them by both the traditions and symbols of their western European colonial education, and the sales talk of the tourist industry that makes dollars from their island. Even Columbus on his fourth voyage, sailing below Trinidad in the narrow channel which separates the island from Venezuela, sensed that he was approaching somewhere special: 'For I believe the earthly Paradise lies here, which no one can enter except by God's leave.'[5] Now, a Grenadian boy writes of his island, using the same image. Like it was for Columbus and Crusoe, his island is a gift of Providence:

> This world it is a Paradise.
> We look at the evergreen trees,
> The sky and the deep, blue seas
> We see the brilliant sunshine that shines so bright.
> And the beautiful stars that glitter at night.
> Shall we forget this Paradise?

Another follows a similar theme:

> Dear Grenada, land of spice,
> To me you are a Paradise . . .

The child develops in this strange elision of genuine response to natural beauty, gullibility to the tourist-trade rhetoric and dream of paradisal perfection. In this context, the world outside his island can become irrelevant to him: his own island becomes his world. The world outside is a different world for him. It is a world of 'continents' and 'cities' and the child may only think of islands. 'What's it like in your island?' the little Tobagonian girl asks the bewildered Canadian tourist, full of the hugeness of his own land and his back strapped up with cameras. To her it is a reasonable question—the world comes to her island and brings its money and its cameras, so it must be the centre, the source of the world. And the sea really is that colour of blue, and the trees that green, and the sand that firm and white. The superficial conditions of the paradisal isle are easily met. But there is also another world inside the beauty:

> Disadvantages of living on an island are the schooling their might be bad because on an island a teacher will get less that she gets in a city. There may not be enough money and in bigger cities there are plenty money. Work might be hard to get. Rich people on an island may treat their servants like slaves just because they know they will stay to get money to send their children to school.
>
> Meat and fish may be hard to buy because people on an island will want money to go away to some city and sell the meat at a high price.
>
> Children may have to walk to school because of bad transportation and cars may not be able to travel on roads because of bad roads, muddy areas and stones.
>
> Children may not get enough to eat and drink and may suffer from malnutrition. People may die easily from the lack of medical attention. Doctors may not attend to the people properly because of their not having enough money to pay him . . .
>
> Thirteen-year-old girl

These are the traps in the paradise, and the anxieties within the garden that make the people reach out from the island world to the outside world, to grasp on to the modernity and the white man's compensations. People wake worried in a clouded paradise:

> *At the Break of Day*
>
> Early in the morning
> When the first cock crows,
> And the grey morning fills the East
> And the fog rises out of the streams:
> Some men sleep on,

But some are already awake,
Thoughtful and worried
Of the coming day.

Thirteen-year-old girl

And if you have no money, there are few respites. This Eden still has the curse of work:

The Dawn of a New Day

When the dawn is peeping
and everybody awakes
To see the bright morning star
Just creeping away.

And the chipper of birds in the air,
And the sun just peeps up from the east
with all its fragrant light
To show the world its pleasant face
with all its golden stripes,

Then people start to stir about
With all their daily toils.

Thirteen-year-old girl

There is an awareness that an island is also a place of labour, sadness, hurricanes and death, where people have lived in total subjection and slavery. There are the prevailing undercurrents of suffering coming through the children's words. The clichés of the gay, dancing, uninhibited West Indian have often been used by the white man to protect his own conscience. Tobagonian children, considering Hemingway's *Indian Camp* as a boy's first discovery of the secrets of life and death, will quickly point out that the young Nick needs to get into a boat and be rowed to an island in order to learn of the intensity of these things. They happen in a special way on an island, they say, there is a special knowledge to be gained there, as if these realities can be seen with more clarity and meaning there, and the child and artist who live on an island will both sense that. It is in this sense that both will see their islands as complete entities, as separate stages of the world.

3

Language and identity

In V. S. Naipaul's story *A Flag on the Island*, Blackwhite, the black writer, rails about the language problem on his island:[1]

'You know Frankie, I begin to feel that what is wrong with my books is not me, but the language I use. You know, in English, black is a damn bad word. You talk of a black deed. How then can I write in this language?'

'I have told you already. You are getting too black for me.'

'What we want is our own language. I intend to write in our own language. You know the patois we have. Not English, not French, but something we have made up. This is our own. You were right. Damn those lords and ladies. Damn Jane Austen. This is ours, this is what we have to work with.'

His indignation is understandable: his identity is suffering. Language itself is the strongest bridge to a secure identity. A feeling that people speak the same language and have the same words for shared ideas is the integrating force amongst them that gives them the feeling of belongingness and trust that society must radiate. A strong, integrating, common language gives the 'social health' that Erikson concerns himself with in his book *Childhood and Society*—a wide faith in the forms and images of society. But when children have a common language that is held to be an inferior one, or a language whose own words and images divide the child from himself, speak against his skin and assert his own subservience, then that same language becomes the destroyer of his identity and the destroyer of his experience. In R. D. Laing's words: 'The choice of syntax and vocabulary are political acts that define and circumscribe the manner in which "facts" are to be experienced. Indeed, in a sense they go further and even create the facts that are studied.'[2] Language can create experience, and political power can control language. For centuries the colonized black man held on to a notion that he was inferior to the white man because the language they both spoke insisted that he was. Of course, he spoke a version of the white man's language in which the qualities of whiteness meant purity and goodness, and the qualities of blackness degradation and devilishness. He experienced his own life in terms of those meanings and images, and believed in them as part of his identity. His language maintained his subservient role in his relationship with the white man, and the definitions of his words vindicated it. Mystification through language is perhaps the subtlest and most insidious technique of domination, and it is still practised on the black man in any country where he speaks a white man's language. A man's language is the strongest factor in his determining of his view of the world and himself. His language translates his world to meaning. His language is his articulated being, is the sense he makes of any aspect of his life and experience. If his language betrays him, his experience is deformed. 'We can be ourselves only in and through our world', says Laing, and when our world speaks division and guilt to us through our language, then we are inevitably divided and guilty.

Between the following two statements, either one capable of being translated into the other, there are two completely different areas of experience, two 'worlds':

It ha' plenty men in Tobago who lime on de street and drink up plenty rum up and down de place. Dey like a whole set of good time and ting.

There are many men in Tobago who meet and talk on the streets, and drink plenty of rum everywhere. They like having good times and enjoying themselves, and going to parties.

In a West Indian island like Tobago, the language tends to divide itself around two standards, both forms of English. There is the local, dialectal, organic English associated with

work, folklore and easy communication. It is often a language
of growth and spontaneous creativity, the language of identity
and belongingness, giving the sounds of a man's essential being
in his own world. It is a black man's version of a white man's
English, and it has often suited the white man's political power
to call it 'Plantation English'. But there is also the other
standard set by the colonial administrators and educators, and
still very much bound up with the class and status of the West
Indian, even as he moves after a new political identity as a
part of a 'Third World' nation. This is the Queen's English, the
white 'received' standard of written and spoken English, a
non-dialectal language, which the aspiring black man, through
his education and mystification, imitates. When he takes the
white man's language he speaks a language of alienation, he
divides himself from the meanings of his words, he begins to
talk, like Blackwhite, of black deeds. A lighter-skinned black
girl will say of a darker-skinned girl, 'She's as black as an
African.' The black man begins to talk of a white man's language
in a black man's world. He exists between two ontologies. As
Derek Walcott, the St Lucian poet, admits, he is perhaps 'Schizo-
phrenic, wrenched by two styles', and the two styles are two
languages, two worlds, two value systems, two opposing
political stances, two skins. To change from one language to
another is to change life itself: 'To change your language, you
must change your life.'[3]

Perhaps in England we have seen a similar problem, but in
terms of class rather than colour. Professor Bernstein has shown
us how a version of language, be it 'restricted' or 'elaborated',
tends to circumscribe the educational chances and lives of
children, and how children who move from one of these codes
to another 'might be restless in their search for belonging'.[4]
They are moving worlds, changing identities. Very often in
West Indian society the accepted categories of colour and class
have elided; yet white men speaking 'Plantation English' are
rare enough. The sociologist Katrin Fitzherbert explains how
the double language standard itself brings its divisions in West
Indian society and in the individual psyche of the West Indian
child:[5]

The syllabus is the crux of the matter, especially as it is

in standard English and the children speak a dialect at
home. It is the most tangible bringer of double standards
into West Indian society. The whole West Indian
educational system is borrowed from England, and its
prizes via scholarships to university are a wide range of
middle class professions in which even black people can
win fame . . . In fact, a working class child has very
little chance of being a success in the wide society
through academic achievements, since it is demanded of
him to excel in terms of a language and culture he only
partially understands.

The Jamaican psychologist, Godfrey Palmer, remembers his
own childhood and education in the context of the violent
shift from one language standard to another that the West Indian child is pressured to undergo, both as a young national
in his own country, and as an immigrant in England:

Superimposed upon his home–school conflict the child
has the additional anxiety of being told that he doesn't
speak English. Unlike the educated West Indian who
knows the difference between standard and Plantation
English, the West Indian immigrant cannot always see
the difference. He becomes insecure and hurt when it is
suggested that he doesn't speak English. His immediate
reaction is one of confusion, suspicion and aggression to
a statement, which, if true, deprives him of the feeling of
belonging that a language confers.

The task involved is not a mere shining and tightening up
of a few grammatical points, or the addition of some new words
and phrases. It is a whole new language and way of life that is
being learned: 'It may be infinitely more difficult for a Jamaican
child to unlearn Plantation English, with its deceptive similari-
ties to standard English, than for a Greek Cypriot child to
grasp the differences between Greek and standard English.'[6]
The double-standard makes for a confused double-vision. In
the context of this shuffling, the identity of the child is uprooted.
He is floundering somewhere between a black and white world.
From feeling relaxed, and possibly unaware of the extent of

his linguistic alienation in his dialectal, organic English, the
new language makes the estrangement from himself a lot
clearer. For the West Indian child as he moves further into his
education, his words become whiter, but his skin is still as black.
And the whiter the words, the more the mystification process
of the language tells him that he must somehow compensate for
his physiological blackness. He must catch up with the white
man. The process becomes more and more insidious, and the
idea of education which implies that a black child, or any child,
speaking dialectal language, must catch up his elaborated white
fellow, is an idea conceived to tear open the identity of the
child. The point goes a long way beyond the racial: 'The pretext
of "catching up" must not be used to push a man around, to
tear him away from himself or from his privacy, to break and
kill him.'[7] Such pressure of alien language and culture on a
West Indian child will often persuade him to throw aside his
dialect and sense of linguistic belongingness, be ashamed of his
island, his past, his skin, his hair and his folklore, and frantically and dividedly to chase after the new elaborated standards
of the second-hand modernity of the white man's compensations: the white skin, the acquisitive life, the divided self.

> And
> Ban
> Ban
> Cal-
> iban
> like to play
> pan
> at the car-
> nival:
> pran-
> cing up to the lim-
> bo silence
> down
> down
> down
> so the god won't drown
> him
> down

down
down
to the is-
land town.[8]

At most West Indian schools, English textbooks are obtained
from England. The children study English language as prescribed
by white Englishmen, and read literature created by white
Englishmen. Often they have been taught English by white
Englishmen like myself. The old colonial preoccupation with
the civil service and bureaucratic administration has made
written received English and 'O' level English language the
imperative qualification for any job involving clerical work in
those islands still drawing from the colonial legacy. 'This
education is a helluva thing', says Biswas, and at its spine is
the General Certificate of Education (Cambridge and London)
English Language examination. Shakespeare, a man much
concerned with problems of the individual's identity ('Who is
it that can tell me who I am?'), gave the situation to his Jacobean
audiences seventeen years before the first efforts to colonize
Tobago. (In 1628 Charles I gave the island, under Royal Charter,
to one of his nobles, the Earl of Pembroke.) The white, colonial
tutor points out his patronage to his slave, telling him how
many linguistic favours he has done him on his own island by
teaching him a new, sophisticated tongue. He does not tell him
the real truth—that a taskmaster and his slave must speak the
same language to make easy the communication of services that
the slave must perform for his master. Prospero speaks to
Caliban:[9]

> Abhorred slave,
> Which any print of goodness will not take,
> Being capable of all ill! I pitied thee,
> Took pains to make thee speak, taught thee each
>   hour
> One thing or other: when thou didst not, savage,
> Know thine own meaning, but wouldst gabble like
> A thing most brutish, I endow'd thy purposes
> With words that made them known: but thy vile
>   race,

> Though thou didst learn, had in't which good
>   natures
> Could not abide to be with; therefore wast thou
> Deservedly confin'd into this rock,
> Who hadst deserv'd more than a prison.

Caliban   You taught me language; and my profit on't
        Is, I know how to curse: the red plague rid you,
        For learning me your language!

Caliban is at least aware of the destructive qualities of the language which he has learned, and it is important to his identity that he keeps his rage alive in that language. He knows, and is angry about his own alienation from the very language that he speaks. He has recognized the process of his mystification by his master. When the island reverts back to Caliban and the colonizer returns home, the language of the old patronage and domination still continues to rule on in his absence. The de-colonized subject will curse on in his ex-master's language. That language is still the currency of communication which buys out the identity of the child as soon as he begins to acquire it.

And Shakespeare himself is a part of the whole English tradition of literature that the West Indian child finds himself immersed in at school. There is perhaps a short play from Shakespeare put on every year at Speech Day, or abridged forms of the comedies and histories: 'The Shrew Tamed', 'An Adventure on Gadshill', 'The Pound of Flesh'—studied from the third form onwards. Then comes 'O' level, and the English teacher finds himself teaching *Romeo and Juliet* before desks of children with black faces:[10]

Romeo   O! she doth teach the torches to burn bright.
        It seems she hangs upon the cheek of night
        Like a rich jewel in an Ethiop's ear;
        Beauty too rich for use, for earth too dear!
        So shows a snowy dove trooping with crows,
        As yonder lady o'er her fellows shows.

Of course, the whole poetic tradition of the white man's language has the roots of its symbolism in the self-vindication and pride

of the user. It must be so, if a language is to speak for the
people who use it. And if they are white, then the language will
naturally vindicate and praise whiteness, and associate it with
concepts such as goodness, innocence, chastity, truth. It is the
colour of the dove, and the colour of love. And so the natural
opposite, the colour of darkness and night, is also the colour of
the 'Ethiop' and the crow. And the whiteness and light domin-
ates, shines out from the darkness. The beautiful, virginal
white girl, Shakespeare's symbol of hope and rebirth, has her
innocence celebrated by her young lover:[11]

> *Florizel*   I take thy hand; this hand,
>   As soft as dove's down, and as white as it,
>   Or Ethiopian's tooth, or the fann'd snow
>   That's bolted by the northern blasts twice o'er.

The blackness is merely the background to the brilliance of the
white and its function is to expose and glorify that whiteness.
The white man's language speaks this. He makes great poetry
out of this. But when the black man speaks it too, he condemns
himself and subserves the white man. The dominant images of
the language that has been hoisted upon him, and which he
continues to adopt, are speaking against him, and gradually
eroding his confidence, whether he realizes it or not.

   And yet white men sitting in their studies an ocean away in
London or Cambridge will give a tick or an extra mark to an
'O' level English literature candidate from a Caribbean island
who scrambles in from rote a quotation like the one above in one
of his answers. If he has absorbed and remembered the statement against himself and his race, and spills it out over his
examination paper, he must get his credit for it. And if he sets
down enough quotations like this one inside two and a half
hours, the chances are that he may pass, and gain more prestige
in his island as it pushes for a new identity as a new nation.
The absurdity of the situation is one liable to constant reoccur-
rence while white man's English is continually set as the language
and literature norm in Caribbean schools. The same problem
will plainly occur in relation to black immigrant children living
in England. The old myths and associations of blackness in the
English language—like rabid sexuality and diabolism—and the

old irrational fears that make the white man close up his heart and mind, will continue as long as the white language and literary traditions are taken literally and seriously enough to make him do so:[12]

> *Iago* Even now, now, very now, an old black ram
> Is tupping your white ewe. Arise, arise!
> Awake your snorting citizens with the bell,
> Or else the devil will make a grandsire of you.

The protective response of some children to write 'BLACK IS BEAUTIFUL' across the cover of their English literature exercise books is plainly the most apt and hopeful comment they can make in such an educational context.

4

English against identity

Prayer of a Black Boy

Lord, I do not want to go into their school,
Please help me that I need not go again,
It's true, they say a little negro ought to go,
So that he might become
Just like the gentlemen of the city,
So that he might become a real gentleman.
But I, I do not want to become
A gentleman of the city, or as they call it
A real gentleman.
I'd rather stroll along the sugar stores . . .

Lord the negroes have had too much work already,
Why should we learn again from foreign books,
About all kinds of things we've never seen?
And then their school is far too sad,
Just as sad as these gentlemen of the city,
These real gentlemen
Who do not even know how to dance by the light of
    the moon,
Who do not even know how to walk on the flesh of
    their feet,
Who do not even know how to tell the tales of their
    fathers
By the light of their nightly fires.
O Lord, I do not want to go into their school again.

Guy Tirolien[1]

In his short story, *Brackley and the Bed*, the Trinidadian novelist Samuel Selvon tells how Brackley, a black Tobagonian, emigrates to England to look for work, and is later pursued there by his old girl friend, Teena. Teena brings the Caribbean with her, and Brackley's English experience soon forces an argument:[2]

'You better go easy with them rations,' he say. 'I not working now and money don't grow on tree here as in Tobago.'

When they was eating Teena say: 'Well you have to get a job right away. You was always a lazy fellar.'

'Keep quiet,' Brackley say, enjoying the meal that Teena cook in real West Indian fashion—the first good meal he ever had in London. 'You don't know nothing.'

'First thing tomorrow morning,' Teena say. 'What time you get up?'

'About nine—ten,' Brackley say vaguely.

'Well is six-o-clock tomorrow morning, bright and early as the cock crow?'

'You don't hear cock crowing in London,' Brackley say.

The story plays out the conflict of some of the opposing factors in the West Indian mind: the opposition between the tropical island life of fruit, fertility and plenitude—the paradisal element—and the English and colonial penumbra of work, money, cities and gloom. As the West Indian child is educated he looks around him, outside his classroom window, and sees lush tropical vegetation, the palms and balisiers, coconut trees, mango trees, bread-fruit, bananas, cocoa. He sees a blue sea, and the sun scorching the red, galvanized roofs of the island's houses. He sees his own world. As he concentrates again on his book he begins to read about another. His mind must be fixed on Europe. In his English textbooks he must read passages and answer questions on, 'We nearly Froze to Death: the story of an Outward Bound Adventure in Scotland', or 'The Coffee-Bar Fashion in London' or 'English Grass Snakes'. He must read about England and white people, in the language of England and white people as he sits inside his black skin on a small island twenty miles away from South America. His situation is culturally absurd. He is mystified, alienated from his own world, his own island. His situation is a concrete image of Laing's statement, 'We educate our children to lose themselves and become absurd.' The child begins to grow up in another world, an alien one to the world around him. It is as if the closest things to him are irrelevant, his whole organic, immediate life a counterfeit, and the English myths and European dreams the only reality that he must know and recognize. The absurdity has come right down from a colonial, expedient situation. In 1847 the Secretary of State for the Colonies had prescribed an idea of education for the colonized peoples, and the influence of his theme still remains. In a despatch he wrote of the English language as 'the most important agent of civilisation for the coloured population of the Colonies', and the purpose for such education lay in the political relationship between England and her colonies: 'the lesson books of the Colonial schools should also teach the mutual interests of the mother country and her dependencies, the rational basis of their connection and the domestic and social duties of the coloured races'.[3] The duty remains. The child must absorb England through the English language. Consequently her life in Tobago is underwritten by the child, she has been mystified into believing that England and the English world she is educated to share form a better, more sophisticated world than her local, organic, Tobagonian one. English habits *must* be better— her whole education and language have indoctrinated her to believe it. Of Brackley's situation in London, she writes this:

> London turns him into a respectable citizen and although
> if he had stayed he might have changed, he would not
> have become so respectable under Tobago's influence.
> London tends to refine many Tobagonians . . .
> Thirteen-year-old girl

The statement is an inevitable comment on her education and alienation from her own world. It is as if she must make this statement, in order to vindicate her European education, and speak out against her own identity.

From the extract *Brackley and the Bed*, Brackley seems

very ambitious, as can be seen when he leaves Tobago to
go to England, which is supposed to be a better place than
Tobago.

'Which is supposed to be a better place than Tobago'—she
hates to say this, she says it reluctantly, sullenly, but her
education has treacherously brought her mind to this point,
taken her towards the conclusion for eight years, and thrown
her out of her own world. The admission has been a struggle,
and it is an admission which she does not want to believe. But
to vindicate herself and her lucrative education it is as though
she *must* believe it. When an extended, concentrated secondary
school education is as rare as it is in Tobago, she cannot afford
to deny the truth of what she learns. But another girl will not
agree. Her own world is still too valuable, too strong for her.
The world of her education is less valid, and her organic life has
kept its primacy. Her identity is more solid, more intact. She
is closer to the values of her own island: she rejects foreignness:

> In Tobago Teena lived a life where she hadn't to worry
> about anything. She only had to do her work, and all was
> well for her. She was accustomed to the lovely beaches
> and the warm tropical sunshine. The big juicy fruits
> especially the mangoes whose sweet juice runs down your
> hand. She was also accustomed to the lovely moonlit nights
> when she can sit under the tall slender palm trees and relax.
> She could not enjoy none of this in England. Instead of the
> lovely moonlit nights and warm tropical sunshine, the nights
> and days were very cold.
>
> Thirteen-year-old girl

She cannot condemn her real life. She can only flow with it,
love it, be it. It has kept its relevance. But with other children the domination of Europe and the alienation process has
been made complete.

> Indolent Brackley carried his West Indian dialect to
> London as if he could not speak better.
>
> Thirteen-year-old girl

V. S. Naipaul has told how his education, in what is considered to be the most desirable of Trinidad schools, forced him to see his own world through the world he read about in English authors like Dickens. It is as if his mind was not allowed to work naturally. It was forced into a foreign, compulsory adaptation. For Dickens's characters:[4]

> I have the faces and voices of people I knew and set them in the buildings and streets I knew . . . Dickens' rain and drizzle I turned into tropical downpours; the snow and fog I accepted as conventions for books . . .

In his novel, *A House for Mr. Biswas*, he tells the story of a man who refuses to see his identity in terms of his organic and immediate life and environment. Biswas only sees the world around him as something unreal. In his worst moments it blurs and becomes a void. The realness is far away from him in England: 'There, where Owad had been, was surely where life was to be found.'[5] He never reaches this realness, and his attempts to climb into the illusion that he can through any 'ideal school of journalism' are sad and futile:[6]

> Mr. Biswas wrote the article on summer; and with the help of the hints, wrote other articles on spring, winter and autumn.
>   'Autumn is with us again! "Seasons of mists and mellow fruitfulness", as the celebrated poet John Keats puts it so well. We have chopped up logs for the winter. We have gathered in the corn which soon, before a blazing fire in the depths of winter, we shall enjoy, roasted or boiled on the cob . . .'

Biswas becomes absurd. His ideals are dissociated from his life, and his mythology from his environment. He is chasing a distant illusion—the English life—which his education and social standards have projected before him. And the problem becomes even greater for Anand, his son, whose education is more intense. He is crammed with Englishness. Biswas's ideal is an illusion, and it is not surprising that books dealing with real experiences of West Indians in England should have such disenchanted titles as *The End of an Illusion* or *The Lonely Londoners*. The West Indians' blackness will allow no playing out of the ideal. Many of the present generation of West Indian school children have sensed this, and their level of acceptance of British standards, subject-matter and examinations is much less enthusiastic than either that of Mr Biswas or Anand. A thirteen-year-old girl's comment on *To Sir, With Love* seems to be tinged with far more reality:

> The girls and boys tried their best to shock Mr. Braithwaite, a new teacher, but soon he was able to understand their aggressive behaviour. Then as he was a black man in England he knew what kind of experience to expect.

In the Trinidadian play *Moon on a Rainbow Shawl* by Errol John, Ephraim, the young Port of Spain train driver, stares at a Union Jack, and holds his dream of England as the escape from the trapped life in a city slum. The end of the play sees him rushing to the docks to catch his boat. The gradual realization amongst West Indians of the English illusion adds the strongest element of dramatic irony to the play. The absurd and depressing nature of the English reliance, starting from education, is becoming much clearer to West Indian children, and its recognition makes them angry and inquisitive:

> . . . In most secondary schools the books used are irrelevant to children. Many of the text books, especially English, are based on aspects of London. The result of this in many cases is that children fail in G.C.E., and are, therefore, unemployed by the Government. This examination is also set by Londoners who look at things from their point of view. I think by importing this examination, the nation reveals that there are no persons in it capable of setting examinations on West Indian aspects.
>
> Fourteen-year-old boy

An important question that is still left to be answered is whether the G.C.E., an exam set by English people for English children should be imposed upon our local children

without consideration as to its suitability for young
people of a young nation.

Fourteen-year-old girl

There is a situation in *Wide Sargasso Sea*, a novel by the
Dominican writer Jean Rhys, where the West Indian girl is
showing the Englishman her island. He looks through his
English eyes at her:[7]

> Then she picked another leaf, folded it and brought it to
> me. 'Taste. This is mountain water.' Looking up smiling,
> she might have been any pretty English girl and to please
> her I drank. It was cold, pure and sweet, a beautiful
> colour against the thick green leaf.
>   She said, 'After this we go down and up again, then we
> are there.'
>   Next time she spoke she said, 'The earth is red here, do
> you notice?'
>   'It's red in parts of England too.'
>   'Oh England, England,' she called back mockingly, and
> the sound went on and on like a warning I did not choose
> to hear.

The Englishman brings his standards and his comparisons to
an exotic island, and they are good enough for him—they work
positively. But they must not be good enough for the children
of that island. They will always work negatively for them. And
black is the colour of the white man's negative.

A Caribbean climate knows no autumn or spring, in the
English sense of the seasons. There is no snow or ice. Walcott
speaks of the 'seasonless climate's dry heat or muggy heat or
rain'.[8] And yet the illusion of England and the European
notion of the seasons and the climate still runs in the mythology
of the children as they live in their villages with English names:
Scarborough, Plymouth, Richmond and Mount Pleasant. At
Christmas they will send each other Christmas cards printed
in England, with snow, holly, robins, yule-logs and Victorian
gentlemen with stove-pipe hats on them. Ask them to draw a
house, and they will often draw a cottage with chimneys. And
outside the classroom the sun beats down and scorches the

grass, and tourists sprawl on the beaches. Their idea of 'Nature'
in poetry is very often purely romantic, fictional and European:

A Trip Through Nature

The rivers wide and gushing down
From snowy mountains high
Meandering along the valleys
Where the water birds do cry.

And the ideal of natural womanhood for the child is a white
man's ideal with the 'long flowing hair' of Europe:

. . . To end this trip through Nature
We speak of man supreme
The female with long flowing hair
And man, the god of beauty's dream.

Thirteen-year-old boy

The boy's own blackness is by-passed, and his own beautiful,
lush world and environment is substituted by a vague and
general world of the imagination, an anaemic Europe. Again,
his education, following these dreams, has been self-denying
and self-alienating. And he uses a typical old-English-textbook-
anthology, conventional poetic rhythm that makes form and
content similarly bloodless. He has been turned away from the
local and the real, and directed to an empty, joyless, predictable surrogate, the one talked about in his textbooks and school
language. If a Tobagonian child is asked to write a poem involving a genuine response to Nature, many times she may come
back with something like this: a pretty cameo of idyllic Europe,
something perhaps that speaks very generally of the foothills
of the Alps:

Spring is Here

Now it is Spring
The trees are blossoming,
The snow is melting from the mountainside
Rivers are flooding the valleys green
Drowning nature's beauty.
Autumn's work has here ceased

The leaves are returning to the branches
And also the beautiful flowers
With fragrance sweet.

This is both a dislocated and fictional vision. The child ignores the real, intense, tropical world around him, to follow after the temperate zones of his European fantasy world. The poem is the obvious consequence of a teaching syllabus which centres around Europe and England, and English cultural traditions. For example, a child will read some extracts from 'In Memoriam', and make these comments:

> This poem is about re-birth of Spring after a long winter, as can be seen from the line:
> '. . . now fades the last long streak of snow.'
> The last verse is a summary of the others, but this time the poet describes himself as being as lively as the awakening of Spring and the budding and blossoming of his heart, which suggest that he is very, very happy and feels much younger as early Spring flowers when they begin to bloom.
> Fourteen-year-old girl

Her remarks are thoughtful and intelligent, and come from a spontaneous response to the poet's mood. Any English teacher would be pleased to read them. But later in the same term, when asked to write a poem about an aspect of her youth, she writes this:

> *Youth*
>
> Oh, how good it is to be young
> To feel the green grass on the ground
> As you kick your shoes off your feet
> To dance helter-skelter on the peat.
>
> To feel the coming of the Spring
> To hear the lively sparrows sing
> As they build their nests in trees,
> Perhaps to get a look at the bees.
>
> So off to the meadows let us go
> To see the first Spring flowers on show

And let us dance, make merry and sing,
We're glad to be young—oh, what a good thing.

The influence here belongs to Tennyson: that is clear. It seems likely that she has assimilated Tennyson's English world and English rhythms and versification as definitely the 'poetical' standards which she must follow. Of course, she has put aside the real world around her, considering it unfit and irrelevant matter for poetry and the expression of experience. It is this kind of education, in fact, that works against the expression of experience, pushing the child towards strange and foreign forms and content. So she tries to express, in unfamiliar language, a world she does not know, and will perhaps never know, and so her poetry itself is lifeless and false. Her vibrant enthusiasm for a blooming countryside has been cramped by alien forms. The child loses her real world, and describes another she will never find. The hope lies in the fact that the same girl can write brilliantly, with truth, and feeling, and insight when she writes of her real world, the world she knows. When she writes of the hurricane she experiences (in the first essay on Hurricane Flora, quoted later), she writes for herself and her world, not against them. But here Tennyson and England have become a part of a mockery of education, a process of self-betrayal and alienation, in which the child assumes that the world that gave her life and sensation is beneath poetical expression, and so she must turn to another which is not hers. This is English against Identity.

Those West Indian poets who have been particularly sensitive to the fragility of their identities in face of pressure from the English-type educations are often forceful in expressing and vindicating the qualities and sensations from their own world in opposition to the temperate, European dream. Here, the Jamaican poet, H. D. Carberry, writes emphatically about Nature and sensation as it belongs to him, as it is wound into his feeling of identity and belongingness to the world around him:[9]

Nature

We have neither summer or winter
Neither autumn nor spring
We have instead the days

When gold sun shines on the lush green canefield
Magnificently.

The days when the rain beats like bullets on the roofs
And there is no sound but the swish of water in the
    gullies,
And trees struggling in the high Jamaica winds . . .

And a fifteen-year-old boy, his childhood home St Lucia, but
now a new immigrant at a comprehensive school in East
London, with a new notion of 'home' and belongingness,
writes about the English seasons as they are, as he knows them,
and walks inside them as a part of his world. His poetry gives
his impressions of this world without idealism or romantic fiction.
The stock images and scenes have also gone with the Tennyson-
ian rhythms and versifications, and the pictures of a lifeless,
predictable world. Now England is a part of his identity, and
not an alien world. His discovery of the London winter is
completely real:

Winters are generally cold and wet and miserable
Like a dog in the rain, or a policeman on his beat,
A time of sitting round your fire and being sad.
A time of watching television and reading and football,
And in the snow, snowballing your friends,
Happy on a sad dark day.

The Forsaken Lover

'My lover is but late today
I wonder what's the matter;
Be it that he no longer cares?
Oh no! he would not cause me tears.

I'll sit and wait, perhaps he's late,
He will not dare to break his date
Those cruel robbers in the square—
Perhaps they've killed my lover there.'

She waited till the evening came
And solemn night approached again,

Till shadows fell softly around
And she could not even see the ground.

She sat there by the window pane
Where she could see both hills and plains,
That if by chance he did come by
She'll be quite sure he did not die.

The sun went down, the stars appeared,
Night's shadow forms were very weird,
Yet there she sat, alone and sad,
To lose him now would make her mad.

She did not sleep a wink that night,
But heard the cock crow for daylight,
Thus many days swept past her there,
She waited for her lover dear.

She mourned with sighing and groaning,
Oh love! Come back to your darling,
O lover dear, why can't you hear?
Sweet mortal, please come near.

Then once she saw a horse galloping
Gliding swiftly over the mountain,
She saw him on the stallion's back
As he rode across the green park,

Hope soared, as he flew towards her,
Her heart reached out to him, her lover,
Then she saw his good companion
Who rode with him on the little stallion.

It was a beautiful maiden
Who had invaded her haven
She didn't want to believe it,
But yet, at least she knew it.

As he approached the little house
His spirit seemed to be aroused,
He hit the horse with all his might
He then shot past her in full flight.

She watched him riding swiftly past,
Her days of love were gone, at last.
He was not dead, but gone for sure,
She had a claim on him no more.

Her heart broke fast and splintered out,
Now she would grieve without any doubt.
Her face grew pale, her limbs grew weak,
Her pretty face was soon tear-streaked.

He married his other lover
And left her alone to suffer,
He had rejected her for sure,
He did not need her any more.

She neither ate, nor drank a sip
To quench the thirst upon her lip
But grief and sorrow was all she knew
As the trees and flowers wildly grew.

Then one day soon the hour had come,
When she, poor maiden, had to be gone,
Her breath was gone, she felt like stones,
While rain and sun did bleach her bones.

Once, later years he did pass by,
And, through the windows he did spy
Yes, she was there, but not his dear.
His love had flesh and she was fair.

Fourteen-year-old girl

I have quoted this poem by a fourteen-year-old Tobagonian girl in full, because I think it crystallizes much of the previous matter of my arguments. Of course, the rhythm and metre are often uncertain and uneven and the events of the last verses somewhat obscure, but the poem's obvious qualities: the starkness of the theme, the honesty of emotion, the violence of the language and the imagery, and the sureness with which she sometimes uses the four-line stanza, make it mature and powerful expression. But the poem, in its context, is a very strange cultural phenomenon. Apart from making the odd gesture to modernity ('He will not dare to break his date'), the black girl in a Caribbean island, composing at night with the crickets and frogs and pans sounding outside in the humid, tropical air, writes within the conventions and structure of the English ballad. She adopts ballad versification and rhythm, the romance legends of wild riders and beautiful maidens, the hills and plains of some fantasy world, the conventional archaisms and rhetorical exclamations, the stock ballad images ('She felt like stones') and the heavy, erotic, masculine idea of the rushing stallion. She even includes a Shakespearian allusion: the 'sweet mortal' is probably due to her study of *A Midsummer Night's Dream*, and Titania's 'gentle mortal' wooing of Bottom. Her class was reading the play closely for 'O' level English Literature during the year she wrote her poem. Her education has stressed to her that this is the way to write poetry: with European themes, environments and myths. The fact that she has been able to produce such a wild and passionate poem inside such alien conventions is an indication of the high merit of her literary skill. Here the fantasy land of the English ballad remains fantasy, remains unreal, and becomes a symbolic land where she can play out her sadness and frustration, a land of the imagination inside her anxiety. There is a very strong sense of the writer's own identification with the forsaken lover herself, and the total sense of loss and decay which she feels, even though she perhaps has in mind a white-skinned maiden. She certainly uses the white image of fatigue and shock when she refers to the 'paleness' of the forsaken lover. The man has found another lover, a 'beautiful maiden', and taunts his old lover by riding past her and callously exhibiting the woman who has replaced her. He is aggressive and pitiless and flaunts his new prize. But the really significant point comes in the last line:

His love had flesh and she was fair.

'She was fair' and the suggestion is obvious, it is written into the child's language and thought, a part of the inevitable and probably unconscious alienation the young girl feels. The new lover is 'fair' and the man has found himself a white lover. The black girl's anxieties and fantasies have suddenly become true. Fair is white, and she is black. Even if the thought was not conscious in her, the language of the self-betrayal and alienation has inevitably made her say it, and once she has said it, she thinks it. It has been said. The white girl is the winner and the black forsaken girl stays in her house and grows old and unloved.

The implication is that the girl, probably without even realizing it, has written herself into a situation of cultural and personal self-denial, and vindication of white people and the white life *merely by using the words that she has always used and she must use*. Merely, in short, by speaking her natural language, made natural by her education. If she doubts that language, she must also begin to doubt her whole way of life bound up inside that language. Her language has made her a loser. It has forsaken her. She has used the language, legends and forms of the white, European world honestly, passionately, and sometimes brilliantly, but they have finally defeated her and left her loveless and lonely. If she is to ever find her lover again, if she is to abandon her own forsakenness, she must leave Europe and its fantasies, ballads and conventions, its white biases. She must come home:[10]

> As I leave Europe
> the irritation of its own cries
> the silent currents of despair
> as I leave Europe
> timid in its recovery and boasts
> I wish for that egoism which is beautiful
> which runs risks
> and my ploughing reminds me of a ship's relentless prow.

5

English for identity?

Rain drips
from the trees
in the dawn;
in the morn-
ing bird
calls, green
opens a crack.
Should you

Shatter the door
and walk
in the morning
fully aware

of the future
to come?
There is no
turning back.[1]

In *The Fire Next Time*, James Baldwin described a situation 'where identity is almost impossible to achieve'. The American negro finds himself born into a world which is not his own, which he can only experience as a white man's world.[2]

This world is white and they are black. White people hold the power, which means that they are superior to blacks (intrinsically, that is: God decreed it so), and the world has innumerable ways of making this difference known and felt and feared. Long before the negro child perceives this difference, and longer before he understands it, he has

47

begun to react to it, he has begun to be controlled by it. Every effort made by the child's elders to prepare him for a fate from which they cannot protect him causes him secretly, in terror, to begin to wait without knowing that he is doing so, his mysterious and inexorable punishment.

It may seem surprising to apply this quotation from the American negro experience to a new nation, Trinidad and Tobago, with a black prime minister and a predominantly black government, but the real governor of the culture—the language—is still in control. The black man still speaks out his experience in words and symbols belonging to the white man, no matter how hard he tries to remind himself and convince himself of the autonomy and dynamism of his own blackness. As soon as the black child acquires his language, he accepts white forms and sees his experience and his own skin through a white focus. And, if the child goes to a secondary school and begins to work towards 'improving' his English, and drops his dialect and organic speech in order to speak 'properly', he moves further and further outside his skin and his island. In Tobago, for example, the 'higher' a child moves in his education, the more distant he often becomes from his roots and his past. He begins to shun them. There follows an unwillingness to accept and consider his local world, the world that has made him. That world often becomes too rustic and retrogressive for him, and sophistication and the modern life seem to lie towards America and Canada, now the English illusion has largely been exploded. His acceptance of his past with its associations with slavery become very hard, particularly when he realizes he is still studying and assimilating in a white man's tongue. He still finds himself in a situation of linguistic colonialism, particularly as the secondary education in Trinidad and Tobago still basically fulfils the old colonial functions of equipping students for the universities abroad and the civil service at home.

The new black intellectuals stress the black man's redefinition of himself in the context of his past as well as his present and future. And if real 'Black Power' is to come, in terms of black people thinking spontaneously as black people in entirely their own psychological context, it can only come organically and naturally if black people adopt a different attitude to the language they speak, a white man's language, which in its use of image, symbol and definition condemns and 'blackens' the name of the black man. The black man must become aware of the extent of his own linguistic alienation. In England, America and the English-speaking ex-colonies, he is assaulted by white norms as soon as he acquires language. As the Boston Schools' Official (a very white man) declared on the subject of English-language teaching to black children: 'We are trying to *break* the speech patterns of these children, trying to get them to speak properly',[3] or trying to get them to speak white by breaking their identities. This is a very violent linguistic process, but as Erikson pointed out, to the white man's notion of history and society the black man's only successful identity has been that of a slave, and it is very often the language that the white man imposes on his black fellows in an area where there is a black immigrant community that is likely to perpetrate such a notion. It is very much like Prospero's trick all over again: give the 'sullen silent peoples' your language, and the debt will stay locked in the consciousness of both sides. The white man calls for gratitude, and the black man curses.

Yet in Trinidad and Tobago, 'correctness' in speech and 'proper' speech are still considered one of the great necessities of a child's formal education. There is the standard of the man who reads the B.B.C. news and also the popularity of Choral Speech competitions, a very widely-subscribed section of the nation's Arts Festivals. This is often judged on the particular group's ability to exaggerate the enunciation of the Queen's English. Vowels are stretched, and consonants savoured, mainly to emphasize the 'correctness' of the speech. A lady writing a letter to a Trinidad daily paper made the following statement:

Sir
I have been making public statements of concern for the language of children—13 and under—in the country. Hence my desire to say publicly that I attended the finals for 'choral speaking' held at the Queen's Hall on the afternoon of June 11th. I was very surprised and overjoyed at the standard of performance I witnessed . . .
    The question I asked myself and others was, why, then, do our youth speak so bad generally? I fear that the

answer is lack of co-operation by other teachers in the
work for 'better speech' being done by a few.

That 'better speech' is the ability to say the 'set poems' picked
by the adjudicators, all of which are particularly engaging for
the glorification of the Queen's English; such as this one set for
children between eleven and fifteen:[4]

Catching Fairies

They're sleeping beneath the roses;
Oh, kiss them before they rise,
And tickle their tiny noses,
And sprinkle the dew on their eyes.

Make haste, make haste;
The fairies are caught
Make haste.

One poem in particular gave the opportunity for an orgy of
vowels that was grasped enthusiastically:

Turtle Soup

Beautiful soup, so rich and green
Waiting for a hot tureen!
Who for such dainties would not stoop?
Soup of the evening, beautiful soup!
Soup of the evening, beautiful soup!
Beau-ootiful soo-oop!
Beau-ootiful soo-oop!
Soo-oop of the e-e-evening
Beautiful, beautiful soup!

And another seemed so foreign to their world as to be completely
bewildering:

'O Mary, go and call the cattle home
And call the cattle home,
And call the cattle home,

Across the sands of Dee',
The Western wind was wild and dank with foam,
And all alone went she.

The one 'local' poem that was used, a poem concerned with
the poor people of Trinidad's slums and shanty-towns, seemed to
have a lot of meaning for the elder children who spoke it. They
found anger and compassion that went a long way beyond flaunt-
ing the 'correct' expression of vowels and consonants in poems
about chasing cows around the River Dee:[5]

History Leaves No Memorials to the Poor

History leaves no memorials to the poor
Dulled by their galvanized dungeons
In the step-steepled Laventille
And the Caroni of their sorrows.

Gravid with anguish and the impossible dream
The poor have always rained
Violent weather on each century's scheme
Of temporal precedence.

Violent in their chaste and holy way,
The poor are never proud of ravishment;
A handsome house, an impertinent fence
An intemperate field and the fastnesses
Of the human heart unleavened by love
Are the same presumptuous fortress above
The virgin and the defenceless poor.

The well-remembered image
Locked in the cycle of the crumbled poor
Is the datum of violence
Compiled by every conqueror
Fouling the past and all our tomorrows.

History leaves no memorials to the poor,
The least-loved and the vanquished,
Dulled in their rising steel cities
And their villages of sorrow;
And nowhere are their names engraved

Among the cherished and the saved,
No monuments of stone
Restore to them their perished humanity.

But all their graves lie open
And day by centuries darkening day,
Someone throws in another primordial bone
Or writes a cheque, or looks the other way.

Marguerite Wyke

Once when we were rehearsing a rendition of Walter de la
Mare's poem, 'The Storm' (a good poem for choral speech, but
a very English one), I emphasized to the group that a good
effect would be to speak one particular line about the seagulls
caught in the storm much louder than the others. 'Say it loud,'
I said, 'say it loud', 'I'm black and I'm proud', they all spontaneously shouted back in unison, as if that theme was a lot
more real and relevant to their needs than Walter de la Mare's
English seagulls.

The tradition of unwillingness to emphasize local themes and
issues in education in Trinidad and Tobago has come under
sharp criticism in the government's latest draft plan for
education in the nation:[6]

Too many persons assume that by making something
relevant to the local scene one is, ipso facto, lowering
standards. This is one of the attitudes which hamper change
and progress, and with which this draft plan is totally
unsympathetic.

The government want their education system to have its
foundation within itself and not rely on Europe, as its people
strive for new identities:

Full national independence and identity will be achieved
and secured only on the basis of an education system which
does not rely on foreign assumptions and references for its
existence and growth.

The new cry is for 'relevance', but the problem really goes

deeper. However relevant the content or subject-matter of the education is to the people of the ex-British West Indian islands, the language and its symbols—the form and vessel of their knowledge—still remain foreign and alienating. There is plainly a certain kind of English, however, into which some children can readily and easily relax. In the story which follows, the sixteen-year-old girl, who speaks received 'proper' English when she is in school and conducting her 'formal' education, writes with a natural and phlegmatic flow, but with a sharp observation and wit, in her dialectal style, producing a real and close sense of experience. She is writing about her own world in unforced words which are a part of her own world:

Time, Thelma and Carnival

It was Carnival Tuesday evening about half-past two and things swinging in town. Bands playing, people jumping and singing and mas' all about the place: Devils, Red Indians, Sailors here, Soldiers there, Zulu Warriors from Africa and in this riot of colour and sound everybody jumping, jumping to the sound of the sweet pan.

Thelma having a ball. Gone for now was the bitterness she feel when they order her to come home half-past six, gone was the hatred she did feel for her grandmother and her mother that afternoon. She thrilling to the sound of the sweet pan and showing it like any Tobagonian.

Thelma was in the fourth form of her school; average height for her age and had enough charm, good looks and brains to catch the boys. She had a long string of girl friends too and now she jumping up with them. They push themselves into the great throng that following 'Our Boys Steel Orchestra' and they jump from Shaw Park to Fort Street and then leave the band and return to the heart of Scarborough to join another one.

On the way down they meet 'Solo Meloharps' going down. Thelma and her friends at once join in. Suddenly Thelma remember the time. 'Anybody have a watch?' she ask her friends, 'Wha is the time?' 'Four o'clock,' came the answer.

'Good,' thought Thelma to herself, 'Ah have two and

half more hours to go and is a good thing because things really hot down here.' And with that Thelma let out a great yell which was lost in all the great noise, and continued jumping like if she mad.

'Solo Meloharps' stop near the bus-stand to let another band pass. Thelma and her friends now in the middle of the band and they frighten because they know when two bands meet all the drunk men always want to pick a fight and then if nobody stop them, it always turn out to be a free-for-all. Then as they half-expect, one of the drunk men in the band that passing throw a bottle into 'Melo-harps' band. Well folks, 'Meloharps' and the supporters of 'Meloharps' didn't like that at all, so they start a fight and all the girls and women start running and screaming and Thelma and her friends get separate. After some time and with the help of some of the supporters of both bands, four policemen manage to quell the fight and carry away the drunk men to sleep it off.

Now Thelma alone. What to do? She ain't have no idea where her friends are or how to get to them. Besides it long after four and good pan music playing and Thelma can't enjoy jumping up by herself.

'You know what it is?' she say to herself, 'I will stand up in front of Sant's Roti Centre and mih friends bound to find me.' So Thelma stand up in front of 'Sant's' alter-nately looking out for her friends and looking at the clock in the window. Half-past four. Nobody. Twenty-five to five. Nobody yet. 'Oh God,' thought Thelma, 'where mih friends? time flying.' Twenty to five. Seventeen to five. Thelma watching the clock more often now. She getting frantic. She toyed with the idea of jumping-up by herself but immediately she know she can't do it. Jump-up by herself? Ridiculous, man. Suppose some fresh man come and hold on to her, what she going to do? Mean-while the minute hand creeping on. Ten to five. Eight to five. Thelma walking up and down now. She can't keep quiet anymore.

'You waiting for somebody, Miss?' inquire a heavy voice. Thelma look up and see a man with a bottle in his hand swaying over her. She ain't even bother to answer; she

just run. Soon she reach Scobie's and there were her friends
waiting for her.

'Girl where you were all this time?' her friends ask her,
'if you know how long we stand up here waiting on you.'
'All you telling me,' answer Thelma, 'I was standing up
just down the road by Sant's waiting for all you. Is a
lucky thing that drunk man chase me or else ah woulda
still be waiting down there. Anyhow wha' is the use
arguing, we find each other, leh we go and jump up nuh?'

So Thelma and her friends move out again. It exactly
five o'clock. An hour and a half more to go. Thelma and
her friends have something else on their minds besides just
jumping up. Something to make the jumping up sweeter.

'Ah wonder where these boys are?' Somebody say,
voicing everybody's thoughts.

'Who woulden want to know?' say somebody else, again
voicing everyone's thoughts.

'Well, who going to miss jumping-up because those
stingy boys ain't here. They mus' be well jumping-up
with some other girls. Leh we enjoy weselves eh,' say
Thelma. This time at the back of her mind, she hope to
see the boys before she go home. The other girls lucky,
they ain't have no old-fashioned mother and grandmother
to tell them to come home half-past six. They could go
home when they want. And again Thelma soul fill with
bitterness. But only for a moment because they had been
threading their way down the road and now they reach
'Symphony Stars' who playing fit to kill. All the bitterness
vanish and she was again full-blooded Tobagonian Thelma.

The happy girls join the band and then, Oh sweet happening! there were the boys that they had been thinking about.

'Sssst' called the boys.

'Play all you ain't here,' say one of the girls, 'they
bound to come and meet us.'

And she right, because in a minute the boys were with
them. 'Where all you were all this time?' demand the boys,
mixing with the girls.

'All about the place,' answer the girls carelessly, trying
to hide their excitement.

Then came the sweetest part of jumping-up. The jumping

boys and girls soon divide into couples and go their own separate way. 'This is living,' thought Thelma to herself. Time was forgotten and Thelma give herself up to the magic of Carnival. Soon it begin to grow dark and the boy at her side hug her closer and Thelma never feel so happy. Gone were the nagging thoughts of time and the warning pictures of her grandmother and mother that had been in her mind all evening.

Thelma and her friend jump down the Milford Road and back up again. They follow a band up Burnett Hill, leave it and follow another one down Fort Hill. They having a grand time. Full darkness descended and the streetlamps gleamed redly on the faces of the sweating mass of people. Thelma ain't thinking about aching arms and feet and worn out shoes.

Sweet pan music playing up Castries Street and of course Thelma and her friend there. They singing 'Ah fraid, ah 'fraid, ah 'fraid pussy bite me . . .' as loud as they could when somebody near Thelma ask, 'What is the time?'

'Half-past eight,' came the answer.

Thelma world gone flat. Her throat dry. Her feet moving woodenly. Half-past eight. Oh God, they would skin her alive.

'I going home, yet,' say Thelma to the boy at her side, 'Ah hungry for so.'

The boy look surprise. 'What you mean you "going home"? The night still young.'

'Nah man,' answer Thelma, trying to keep her voice steady. 'I going home, ah hungry too bad.'

'Oh God, you think ah go starve you. Ah go buy something for you to eat.'

'Oh gosh man, doh argue with me, nuh. When I hungry, I real hungry and nothing could full me up but good food.'

'Allright then,' say the boy, determine for her not to spoil his night, 'Ah go walk you home.'

Thelma see he determine and allow him to walk with her. Thelma set up a fast pace, listening with only half an ear to what her escort was saying. 'Why you walking so fast?' ask the boy. Thelma think fast. 'You ain't feel

rain?' she ask, 'It feeling like rain go fall.' This time
Thelma frighten for so. The boy ain't say anything, he
just match he pace to the girl own. When they about two
hundred feet from the house Thelma say, 'I think you
better turn back here. If mih mother see you she going to
be vex.' 'More vex than she is now', added her mind.

'Allright,' say the boy, letting go her hand, 'Goodnight
Thelma. See you in school tomorrow.'

Suddenly Thelma can't walk fast anymore. She drag
her feet the last hundred yards. Is a different Thelma who
creep in by the gate and let herself quietly through the
backdoor and into the kitchen. She ate without any
appetite, the supper that they leave for her. She eating slow,
slow because she want to put off the quarrelling that she
sure coming to her. Soon she finish however, and reluctantly she leave the kitchen for the dining room.

As she reach the door, her mother come through it.
She begin quietly as always. 'Where you were all this time
Thelma?' Thelma ain't answer. She know better than to
open her mouth. And then her mother begin to blow all
colour bubbles. 'Look at the time and you now come home.
Half-past six, ah tell you to fin' you' self home here and
now is after nine and you just reach home. What kinda
young woman you going to be? You doh have respect for
nobody.' And so she go on and on for a whole half-hour.
All about how she getting own way and how she so rude
and about past carnivals and about last year Christmas
when she break the nice, new vase. She finally and with,
'Anyhow, is the las' time you going and jump-up. Is the last
time you even going in town Carnival day. Now pass and
find you' self in you bed before ah come in there.'

Thelma pass fearfully receiving a box to help her on
her way. She pass her grandmother who just look at her
in a suspicious kind of way and say not a word. She feel
even worse, because although she was feeling hate for her
grandmother that afternoon, she really love her plenty.

Thelma go into the bedroom and change her clothes and
get into bed. She smile to herself in the darkness. The
sting of the slap and the quarrelling already wearing off.
She know her mother say that she wasn't going back in

town another Carnival day, but then she always making
those kind of threats. Besides next Carnival far, far off.
'Carnival tough, tough, tough,' say Thelma to herself, as
she go over all the events of the past evening in her mind.
Then because she so tired, she soon fall into sweet sleep,
sure, sure that the very next Carnival she would be again
in the heat of things, jumping and thrilling to the music
of the sweet pan.

This is real Tobago: the humour, the boisterousness, the humanity, the flowing with the self. England is forgotten. Established
'properness' is lifted away, and genuine sensation and love throb
through the writing. Perhaps this is English for Identity.

The insipid poetry taken from a stereotyped European
fantasy world turns into something dynamic and experiential
when the child takes his words from the reality around him.
He looks at the setting of the tropical sun, perhaps in the context of the war-scarred history of his island:

> The sky's all blood, like a battlefield
> With its soldiers all wounded, praying to be healed.
>
> Fourteen-year-old boy

A girl remembers the aftermath of a hurricane:

> With a sullen, sonorous sound
> The hurricane died down,
> Only bits and tins
> Left as mark of its sting.
>
> Thirteen-year-old girl

She thinks of some friends leaving her island, perhaps emigrating
to England or Canada:

> It was their last visit
> We were all standing, close together
> With our minds based on each other
> Saying farewell.

Down the close, darkening road
They made their way
With faces grimly gay
Saying farewell.

They boarded the ship
Without looking back . . .

Another poem speaks of the sea, of its fury and inconstancy,
using a strange vision of men salvaging a wrecked ship. The
weird empathy the child has with the sea, how it lives and
breathes and becomes suddenly murderous, comes through his
own unique sensations of his own world, moving through his
language and creating a timeless sense of menace:

Ship Wreck

From dawn till dusk they laboured;
But only a few things they had salvaged.
The twisted wreckage of the boat loomed
Silently in front of the shipwreckers.

The shipwreckers were sore and hungry
But there was no time to eat.
They heaved and puffed and laboured
They wondered when they will be released
From this ordeal.

The sea was calm as though unaware
Of what was taking place.
The men heaved a casket of wine which
Slipped and dropped.
As if by chain reaction the sea roared
Its disapproval.

The sea swelled and crashed
And, as if inhaling, took in the men
And vomited their water-logged
Bodies on the golden sand.
                              Thirteen-year-old boy

English is the linguistic accomplished fact of the ex-British islands of the West Indies, and it has been established as the language of the people, black or otherwise, in islands like Trinidad and Tobago. The previous poems illustrate that a child can very often write unselfconsciously in English, and really express the sounds and experience of his own world. But very often the themes of the mature West Indian writers like Naipaul, Brathwaite, Walcott and Jean Rhys have concerned the search for identity, the sensation of rootlessness and the feeling of isolation. It is as if they have been trapped inside these themes, and have always been nagged to pursue them: Brathwaite's long poem *Rights of Passage* tends to see the problem as a purely black one:[7]

> Where then is the nigger's
> home?
>
> In Paris, Brixton, Kingston,
> Rome?
>
> Here?
> Or in Heaven?
>
> What crime
> his dark
>
> dividing
> skin is hiding?
>
> What guilt
> now drives him
>
> on?
> will exile never
>
> End?

His theme is the uprooted black man, floundering around the world, looking for a place which will somehow connect with him:[8]

> Ever seen
> a man
> travel more
> seen more

lands
than this poor
land-
less, harbour-
less spade?

It is the 'dark dividing skin' of Brathwaite's black man that pushes him endlessly forward. Divided from his language and symbols—the property of a white skin—it can only harass and torment him. But the feeling of rootlessness cuts across specific racial identities: Brathwaite's Barbadian negro, Naipaul's Trinidadian Indian—even the white woman on the wildest island, seeing her whiteness as the cause of her isolation ('I wanted to be black. I always wanted to be black'), makes her own voyage in terms of a young creole chorus girl in England, moving on from dark, wet city to city, room to room, her consciousness wavering between her island and the new country that has always been the country of her speech and dreams:[9]

> Sometimes it was as if I were back there and as if England were a dream. At other times England was the real thing and out there was the dream, but I could never fit them together.
> After a while I got used to England and I liked it all right; I got used to everything except the cold and that the towns we went to always looked so exactly alike. You were perpetually moving on to another place which was perpetually the same.

A great writer—like Naipaul—who writes in a language foreign to his roots and his skin, a language which is not his, but in fact has to be his because it is the one he acquired as a child, will inevitably find himself writing about problems of isolation and identity, alienation and rootlessness. His identity was somewhere 'out in the void, beyond the dot of Trinidad',[10] in an area of darkness. His 'home' was a Caribbean island. His ancestors were Indian indentured labourers. And he speaks the language of England. The childhood innocence of sensation and impression into which the child relaxes before the consciousness of his dividedness, disappears. The mature writer, it seems, is locked inside his identity problem. A conscious preoccupation with 'identity' will inevitably become the object of his art. His language, itself a foreign factor, forces this. A writer must feel good, easy, relaxed in his language, must be sure that it is his own language, before he can escape the feeling of unsureness and alienation which a strange language and culture of unbelongingness brings. But Naipaul shows that great literature can be squeezed out of the taut tensions generated by the dislocation between language and identity. His novel *The Mimic Men* is perhaps the culmination of this tormented feeling. As a vision of the disorder and ruins of a man's own identity, it is stark and horrifying. The 'hero', examining his own devastation, has 'contracted out' of his own and anyone else's identity: 'A man, I suppose, fights only when he hopes, when he has a vision of order, when he feels strongly there is some connexion between the earth of which he walks and himself.'[11] But those connections are formed and expressed in and through his language, and it is imperative that his language reflects him and his own world, that it does not continually betray and humiliate him by the meanings and pressures of its dominant images.

Naipaul said of black writers in America and the West Indies that they tended to trap themselves inside their blackness, and were very often only interested in taking sides and winning acceptance of their racial group. Blackness 'cannot be the basis of any serious literature', he said. He goes on to emphasize in *The Middle Passage* that the West Indian world has no strong framework of social convention, and can only borrow from the white world: 'the only convention the West Indian knows is his involvement with the white world. This deprives his work of universal appeal.'[12] But it is the wider world in terms of the white world. There is Naipaul himself, or Brathwaite, fulfilling in their own lives the metaphorical search in their novels and poetry: going back to India or Africa, pushing back into their pasts to find roots and meanings that are all transcribed in their art through the white man's tongue. But the West Indian negro's Africanness, Naipaul's Indianness, Jean Rhys's whiteness, all contaminated and afflicted as they are by the Englishman's language, lead the West Indian on more and more to search for his identity in the face of its elusiveness, giving him a continuous metaphor for his journey, taking him further into the most universal of problems.

In the context of this massive preoccupation with identity in West Indian writing, the arguments against the present structure and material of English education in the West Indies are obvious: the irrelevance of much of the subject-matter, the bad examination system which gives power of pass and fail to obscure examiners in England who may know nothing of the West Indian ethos, and the lack of confidence in local themes. If one considers these disadvantages inside the alienating force of the language that teacher and child speak, there is plainly much that needs changing. The main problem seems to be: how do you make black children aware of the dangers of the language which they speak, without stunting their usage of its communicative, creative and enduring qualities? My main contention is that such a child *must grow up on English as spoken by his own people inside the society which is to be his,* rather than English as spoken by Englishmen. He already is inside a great literary tradition, and even now there is enough substantial West Indian literature to furnish both a profound and varied English school curriculum at all ages and levels. If he is to read English literature by English authors, he should see it in the context of his own West Indian literary tradition and not vice versa. He should not be sold the English tradition before he knows and has explored his own. If he is to study Shakespeare, it should be in the context of his own world and his own writers' use of English. He should not be given the odd token gesture of Caribbean literature in the surrounding context of Shakespeare, Wordsworth and Jane Austen.

His education must place him in a tradition of his own, and give him the secure sense of cultural belongingness that every person needs as a basis to think and act. His knowledge of himself and others must come inside a feeling of sharing a common literary identity inside his particular world and people. Education inside any other foreign culture means dependence and subjection to that culture. It is the way back to colonialism and absolute reliance on alien standards controlled by foreign people. And to the black man, white standards of language and culture are essentially oppressive standards which maim and destroy his belief in himself. George Jackson (*Soledad Brother*, p. 30) looked back to his own school life and concluded:

> I know now that the most damaging thing a people in a colonial situation can do is to allow their children to attend any educational facility organised by the dominant enemy culture.

The same kind of awareness is happening at the classroom level in Trinidad and Tobago. In the *New Beginning*, the newspaper of the Trinidad and Tobago Co-ordinating Committee, a black student wrote, 2 April 1971:

> Another fact which the system seems to overlook is that the bulk of students are black and the education which we receive is white. The result is a black student with a white mind. With his white mind the black student completely forgets his colour and enters white society . . .
> The whole cause for the shortcomings in our educational system is the G.C.E. We allow those 'beloved' Englishmen to set our standard of Education for us. We allow them to dictate what we must and we must not learn, when it would be in their interest to keep us ignorant.
> . . . It is quite clear that Mr Cambridge and Mr Oxford cannot begin to know a thing about our society . . .

In Trinidad and Tobago the General Certificate of Education examination, prescribed and marked in England, holds even more significance than it does in England. Any clerical work or civil service post requires 'O' level English language (the ability to communicate like an articulate white man), and there is often a hostile desperation for a West Indian child to pass the examination that makes him turn to private tuition and frantically write after Wolsey Hall correspondence courses. In a country where so many young people are unemployed and a job in the Government Service or Banking seems to represent the change from labourer to civilized man, 'O' level English language becomes like a guiding star. It exerts a depressingly huge influence as a token of acceptance into the white man's standard of expression and culture. As such it becomes an important weapon of white domination and black estrangement. The academic future of the West Indian is still decided in Oxford and Cambridge. Without his 'A' levels he cannot gain admission even to his own Caribbean university. The colonial structure still controls any educational progress the West Indian tries to make.

This situation becomes even more absurd when the power and many-sidedness of so much Caribbean culture is examined. There is no need to argue the merits of Caribbean literature. Is there a better novelist in England than Naipaul? Are there better poets than Brathwaite or Walcott? These writers should be read and studied closely in English schools as well as in the Caribbean: English people, black and white, have so much to learn from them. And there is the whole tradition of Black American literature and African literature, with books about growing up black in a white man's world, the awakening consciousness of the black child in that world: Richard Wright's *Black Boy* or Camara Laye's *The African Child*.

But it is the G.C.E. structure which sets the syllabus and cultural direction, and as long as it continues to exist in the Caribbean, that direction will always be towards England. Everything that he reads tells the child that his educated eyes must stare longingly towards England. His own island, his education tells him, is not a place for the intellectual. Education means exile, even when you sit in your Caribbean classroom. Why set *The Long and the Short and the Tall* for 'O' level, a very 'English' play reliant on much of its dramatic power on the strong interplay of regional British dialects, when there is an excellent play in *Moon on a Rainbow Shawl* set in Port of Spain, and very skilful in its use of Trinidad themes, dialects and speech rhythms? Why teach *Jane Eyre* for 'O' level when there is a very fine Caribbean sequel in *Wide Sargasso Sea*? Why study novels about problems in English society when sharp social commentary on West Indian themes can be found in books like Mittelholzer's *A Morning at the Office*, or Patterson's *The Children of Sisyphus*? Why study Mark Twain, Jules Verne, John Masefield or Jack London in the first and second years when there are novels for younger readers like Namba Roy's *Black Albino* or Andrew Salkey's *Hurricane*? And there is the work of Wilson Harris, Lamming, Hearne, Selvon and Lovelace. Any arguments for continuing with a dominantly 'English' English would seem very slight with such an impressive Caribbean output. And in his excellent anthology of West Indian writers for school children in the Caribbean, Kenneth Ramchand has this to say about the teaching of literature in Caribbean schools:[13]

> But there is also a positive indifference to literature on the grounds that it is neither enjoyable nor useful. It is seen as the worst of school subjects, something which has to be learnt, but which, after all the trouble, has no connection with one's own life and interests, a bookish subject which is useless as soon as one leaves school . . .
>
> These attitudes originate and are consolidated in the schools. For the student, literature has generally meant English Literature, which is set in a foreign country, which contains English characters and English situations and which, in many ways, is rooted in English life and manners. It is possible to read and enjoy this literature, but the younger reader may find it difficult to see beyond what he takes to be its Englishness.
>
> The local details in geography and culture are often outside his experience, and sometimes difficult to imagine: whereas these details usually function in an unobtrusive way for the English reader, the West Indian student is constantly distracted by their foreignness and novelty . . .
>
> The foreignness of English literature operates to the disadvantage of literature in another way. Some of the situations which arise in English fiction are not immediately relevant to the West Indian student or to the society of which he has direct experience. The student therefore rarely becomes involved, and what is probably worse, he begins to build up the attitude that literature has very little connection with life and society.

His remarks are easily supported by the apathy and bored faces of the Tobagonian children reading *Short Plays from Shakespeare*, or *A Journey to the Centre of the Earth*, and the very different interest and enthusiasm radiated for his own anthology, particularly for stories like *Kanaima*, by Wilson Harris, with its setting amongst the Amerindians in the Guyanese jungles, or *Brackley and the Bed*, with the strong humour of the West Indian's London exile.

> they go to school to the head-
> master's cries,
>
> read a black-
> board of words, angles
>
> lies;
> they fall
>
> over their examinations.
> It is a fence that surrounds them.[14]

It is plain that mere relevance, or a shift in focus from the London streets to the Caribbean palm trees, is not enough. The problem goes beneath the locale and themes in the literature of the language itself. The damage is done there. The English teacher in the Caribbean must be assiduous in explaining to his students, as their capacities for criticism develop, the dangers of the language which they speak. A black child should never be expected to unquestionably accept the symbolic meanings of black and white in the English language based as they are on the vindication of whiteness and the degradation of blackness. Such a language speaks against him and lies about his beauty, his hopes and his realness. He should be introduced to a consideration of the way in which the white man uses these symbols, and how he may possibly find himself using them. He must not accept the white man's lies against him, lying as they do in the very basis of the symbolism of the language, and neither must he unwittingly lie and malign himself. If English has become his language, then he must speak it, but it must not destroy him or drive him from himself. Such expression and sophisticated language like the previous quotations from Shakespeare should be critically examined and discussed, so that the child begins to take on awareness and knowledge, not dividedness and guilt. Why should black have these meanings? What does the adoption of the white man's language mean in his life? How far does it compel him to strike an apologetic tone for his blackness:

Morocco   Mislike me not for my complexion,
             The shadow'd livery of the burnish'd sun,
             To whom I am a neighbour, and near bred.[15]

He will begin to see that there may be strong and extreme
differences between the way in which the white world sees him
and speaks about him, and the way in which he will choose to
see himself. When he has discovered this he will know that it is
his own view and the view of his own people that matter in the
passage of his life, and he will begin to control a language and a
world capable of enclosing and defeating him. He will begin to
see that there are other times when black means beautiful and
white is the colour of snow and coldness and skin as 'white
as leprosy'.[16]

> A teacher read,
> He read on and on
> About colour,
> I just glared
> The period ended
> He demanded to know what I was
>   glaring at,
> I told him
> I was admiring his arctic colour.
> He glared more,
> And shouted me down to the head.
> The head quietly asked what happened.
> I told him everything, the teacher's
>   part and mine.
> He replied,
> Saying it was his job
> And that I had a point too.
> He said again he'll just give me one.
> I told him there was small justice,
> For saying that I got two.
>
> Fourteen-year-old boy

And when it is also the insidious whiteness of the whale:

. . . yet for all these accumulated associations, with what-

ever is sweet, and honourable, and sublime, there yet lurks
an elusive something in the innermost idea of this hue,
which strikes more of panic to the soul than that redness
which affrights in blood.

This elusive quality it is, which causes the thought of
whiteness, when divorced from more kindly associations,
and coupled with any object terrible in itself, to heighten
that terror to the furthest bounds . . .

Herman Melville: *Moby Dick*

He will begin to find new symbols which speak of him, not
against him. He will make changes in his language. He will find
his own 'English' which is not English, and break the white
confines around his words and mind. He will write in the way
most 'proper' to him—the way which tells of his own world and
himself.

But this can only be achieved if the shift of standards, criteria
and focus from London to the Caribbean is managed. While
London still rules West Indian education by her examinations,
textbooks and literary standards, any hopeful notion of the
autonomous political or cultural power of blackness in Caribbean
communities remains futile and stillborn.

6

Drama and identity

> To educate man to be ACTIONAL, preserving in all his
> relations his respect for the basic values that constitute a
> human world, is the prime task of him who, having taken
> thought, prepares to act.[1]

> No, we do not want to catch up with anyone. What we
> want to do is to go forward all the time, night and day,
> in the company of man, in the company of all men.[2]

'Identity' itself, the feeling of belongingness, is the most necessary feeling that any individual needs in any society, but when
a new nation is asserting her own newly-wrought independence
as a new political entity, the notion of 'Identity' amongst its
young people will have a special importance. These are the
people who will be responsible for maintaining that hard-won
concept of national identity, and it seems necessary that their
English education, through essays, discussion and debates,
should suggest to them exactly what that means. Not in any
doctrinaire approach, but merely by stimulating an awareness
of their own nation's aims and means of government in the
context of world organizations and movements. It seems
absurd in itself that any school 'subject' concerned with
Caribbean life, culture and Identity should still be called
'English'. Perhaps the subject would carry less weight of
alienation if the name itself was changed.

But the idea of political awareness as a part of their 'literary'
education is particularly important for ex-colonial peoples who
have lived for long periods with subjection, and have often come
to accept it in the same way that they have accepted and adopted

the white man's language. The awakening awareness of the linguistic colonization which still oppresses them has a strong alienating effect which could possibly create either a very aggressive attitude to the white world and its forms and cause them to curse like Caliban in the white man's language, or it could induce a high level of apathy and cynicism which would have a deadening effect on their consciousnesses both as individuals and nationals. There is still the feeling amongst many black children in the islands that if they had the power and choice, they would rather be white. This is the consequence of the symbols they have always used in their language which say, in short, that it is better to be white. So then the black child will be on the defensive to protect his skin, in the face of the accusations made about it by the language which he and the white English world both speak: 'It's not my fault I'm black,' he says, 'and anyway, what's wrong with being black?' These undercurrents of self-defensiveness very often show themselves when a black child considers that either he or his race has been wronged. And then even by protecting himself, the white words which he uses will accuse him again, and apologize again for his blackness. A fourteen-year-old Tobagonian girl wrote this in an essay on student militancy:

In Sir George Williams University in Canada, many
negroes are being repeatedly failed in their examinations.
This should not be. Man likes to own and be master, he
likes to be powerful and important. These being man's
chief qualities, if he knew that white would be the ruling
colour, and he was responsible for the colour of his skin, he
would surely have it changed to white. But he is not to
be blamed for being black, then why should such unjust
penalties be imposed on him?

From this tone of passivity, forced upon her by the power of the white bias of the language she has to use when referring to 'colour' differences, she changes to something more positive:

A professor had deliberately failed a Negro student because
of his colour, and passed an English student on presenting on
a duplicate of the Negro's work.

Such acts of injustice only raise the colour barrier higher.
They impose upon the negro population great hatred for
the white population. No man would sit back and be
cheated without fighting for his rights.

The economic plight of the West Indian is stressed. His lack of
money for a university education, just like his language, throws
him back on the favours of white people and compromises his
skin, his dignity and his independence. And the girl has to
retreat again when she comments on the militant action of
mistreated West Indian students at a Canadian university.
The language plight and the economic plight elide. Both areas
are dominated by whiteness, and the black child steps down:

The negroes exhibited their bad manners and long-
restrained rage by this vicious action. It was one of the
worst possible things they could have done and it would
have some very bad effects on the younger people who are
hoping to enter a university.

Now that these misfortunes have arisen, there would be
little or no chances of any negro entering the Canadian
university in future. Negroes would no longer be trusted
or accepted by the Canadian Government. The Canadian
Government would no longer give negroes scholarships to
their universities.

The girl's concluding analysis of the world problem between
black and white suggests the nature of the struggle almost in the
way that Fanon saw it: the white man consolidates and continues
the politics of domination because of his fear of the black 'take-
over', whereas the black man of the 'third world' tries to improve
his conditions in his own cultural context, away from the
domination of Europe, and asserts his own culture in the face of
inevitable comparisons:

It is more likely than not, the white man is deliberately
suppressing the black man for his own selfish reasons. He
is afraid of losing his power and wealth to the black man,
while the black man is desperately struggling to improve
his present conditions.

If every one explored the main objects of these turbulent uprisings, they would find no other reason than racial discrimination as the cause. If only racialism can be dispelled from these societies, these problems would be overcome. This is the only alternative, since black and white men would always exist.

'Since black and white men would always exist.' But how to make them coexist without the white domination of the black, particularly in an education situation where the black man speaks the language and unwittingly asserts the symbols of the white world? The poetical answer seemed to be to make the world, white and black and yellow, come to Tobago, so it became the political centre of the world, the stage of world affairs, as it must be for the children who are going to live there and find their identity with the island. If it is a fiction that Tobago is the centre of the world, it is not a fiction that Tobago is the centre of the world for Tobagonians. For Tobagonians, the world must unashamedly be seen in the context of Tobago, from the standpoint of Tobago. So the world came to Tobago in the form of mock 'United Nations General Assemblies', organized to provide a theatrical and humorous experience, as well as a politically earnest one. For a few afternoons Tobago became the world's political platform and stage.

The prime mover in the 'assembly' became Trinidad and Tobago. The Trinidad and Tobago delegate, assuming the garb and deaf-aid of the Prime Minister, Dr Eric Williams, initiated the 'Draft Resolution', and was the first speaker to vindicate it. The resolutions were drawn up with a great deal of seriousness, normally at the time when the issue involved (for example Rhodesia, Anguilla) was at some climax of world affairs. Here is a part of the resolution used for the 'assembly' on the Rhodesia problem:

Draft Resolution moved by Trinidad and Tobago

Realising that the Universal Declaration of Human rights is a common standard of achievement for all peoples and nations.

Having considered the report of the special committee on

the policies of Apartheid of the Government of Rhodesia.

Convinced that the situation in Rhodesia and South
Africa continues to pose a threat to International peace
and security.

Considering it essential to promote a closer and greater
co-ordination of international efforts to eliminate Apartheid
and racial discrimination in Rhodesia,

The Government of Trinidad and Tobago

(1) Reiterates the condemnation of the policies of Apartheid practised by Rhodesia as a crime against humanity.

(2) Reaffirms the recognition of the legitimacy of the
struggle of the people of Rhodesia for human rights
and fundamental freedoms for all of the people of
South Africa irrespective of race, colour or creed.

(3) Strongly reiterates its conviction that the situation in
Rhodesia constitutes a threat to international peace
and security, that action under chapter 7 of the Charter
of the United Nations . . .

The children made their contributions with great conviction,
each one representing a specific nation involved. They had
examined the policies of the particular nations they represented,
and now assumed the normal attitudes of their nation to such
a resolution in their speeches. There was some unlikely and
sharp humour: bomb scares, assassination attempts, Arab–
Israeli bombast and outside demonstrations, and the boy who
played the South African delegate appeared with his face
blanked out with flour. But it was also very much of the politics of sympathy and experience:

Firstly, the policy of Apartheid needs condemnation
because it entails separation and 'separation' is an ugly
word . . . Let me give you some insight as to the gross
discrimination practised in Southern Rhodesia. I was
flying to Zambia, but in order to break the long journey,
my plane stopped at an airport in Salisbury, and Mr.
President, I was denied lunch because I was the sole
negro. It was a long, very long trip, tired and hungry I
was, but incredibly enough, I did not eat. On this trip, I

also learnt that Negroes are not allowed to try on or touch
material in stores—probably it is thought that when the
negro comes into contact with the cloth, a disease will be
passed from the negro to the cloth. Negroes are forbidden
to enter bars and drink rum at a place called Lusaka in
Northern Rhodesia. A negro to whom I was speaking on
my last visit to Rhodesia announced:
    'We don't want permission to enter the whiteman's bars,
what we want is proper education, and to have a say in
affairs of government—the white man still thinks of us as
children.'
    There it is, Mr. President, the Rhodesian European still
thinks of the average negro in terms of the African negro
imported to the West Indies about 400 years ago!

Fifteen-year-old girl

The black child in the Caribbean island becomes the African
again, goes back to her roots and, in her imagination, begins to
know and feel Africa again, and the trials of her fellows there.
Her identity leaves Europe even further behind, and moves towards both a confirmation of itself, and a fusion with the other
peoples of the third world.

When I was hungry, you fed me books, Daniel's dungeons
now I am thirsty, you would stone me with syllables.

We seek we seek
but find no one to speak

the words to save us.[3]

Perhaps Brathwaite's words point to the conscious or unconscious levels of bitterness that a black West Indian child may
have towards the words he is compelled to speak at his school.
They are words which do not 'save' the speaker, but condemn
him against himself. It seemed imperative to try to get the
children writing and acting from their own experience, and not
a borrowed, colonized one, in the language and style of movement which gave them most ease. But in Tobago there was often
a sense amongst the children that they must turn aside from

their own world, to shun things local, and stretch after the
world which seemed to form the approved subject-matter for
the 'proper' language stressed in their schools. Many of them
were the sons and daughters of middle-class civil servants and
shopkeepers—themselves very much intimidated by, and
sucked towards what Naipaul calls a dream of 'modernity' in
The Middle Passage, the reaching after the 'modern' world of
Europe and America with their seductive domestic technology
and fashions. The tradition at school had always been to act
out a short play from Shakespeare at most speech days, together
with other contributions by the choir and dance group. The
Shakespeare play had given them the chance of dressing up in
exotic foreign costume (itself a very important part of the
ritual of the yearly Carnival), to make themselves up and to
speak out good and proper super-enunciated language, and
generally display their level of acceptance and assimilation of
the white man's English and theatrical deportment. The suggestion that perhaps we should try to act a play with a more
relevant and 'local' theme was greeted with horror by some girls,
who immediately dissociated themselves from any such produc-
tion. A play on a local theme set in a fishing village at the time
of Hurricane Flora, which devastated the island in 1963, seemed
to some of the girls only to be about 'a lot of old fishermen', and
was hardly the elevated subject for a speech day drama. The
theme seemed too local and rustic for them. It was as if their
education was designed to enable them to escape from these
things, and to concentrate the educational focus on their own
island and world was an unnecessary and retrograde step.

The idea behind such a play came after the children had
written in class essays some earnest and eloquent accounts of
the hurricane as they had experienced and remembered it. We
were also reading some excerpts from Andrew Salkey's novel
Hurricane at the time in class. Salkey's novel is set in Jamaica
and is very successful in expressing the real, instinctive responses
of a young boy towards the sudden and violent upheaval of
normal life. The children were asked to write an essay concern-
ing an aspect of danger and violence that they would remember
in their lives. Many of them responded by describing their own
experience of Hurricane Flora, plainly a critical event in their
lives when their childhood life underwent a sudden and violent

disruption in the context of suffering, perplexity and death, all dominating the atmosphere of tragedy:

> The sun rose in a very clear sky. I awoke with a feeling that something very unusual was going to happen. I think it was because of the dream I got the night before.
>
> At nine-o-clock, grey dismal clouds started to form in the sky and I had not left for school as I could get no transport. The rain began to fall and I gave up all hopes of getting a vehicle. I was just about to go home, when a car stopped and offered to take me to my school, which was twenty miles from where I lived.
>
> That morning I reached school one hour late, much to the disapproval of myself and my teacher who is a lady who likes strict discipline.
>
> At eleven-o-clock the rain was still pouring heavily. The seas were behaving as if they had a monster. The waves crashed on the beaches. The little boats that were in the sea started dashing about and many were destroyed by the thundering waves.
>
> Church bells started ringing, the sirens started screeching, and it was then that I realised that we were about to experience our first hurricane in decades. The children were very panicky when they heard the news. Many cars came to take home their usual passengers.
>
> As I was living very far from school, I had to wait until the evening when my father came to take me home. Many of the children had left by twelve-o-clock, and very soon there were only nine children (who like me were living far), who were left in the school.
>
> The school-house was a very old building. Two little girls were playing hide-and-seek, unaware of what was going on. One of them went to hide below a bench near a window. It so happened that as soon as she was about to come out of her hiding place, the partition by the wall caved in and pinned the little girl to the floor. Her friend saw her fall, but being a little girl, she stood watching.
>
> I was upstairs with the other girls and I noticed that I was not hearing the little girl's laughter. We descended the stairs and as we touched the landing, the girl who

was watching ran to me and started maundering and pointing frantically towards the caved-in partition. After a minute she fainted in my arms. The other girls ran over to the partition and freed the girl. She opened her eyes, watched us, and then shut her eyes as though she had fainted. By that time I was really frightened.

An hour later my father came for me and he took her to the hospital, where she died on arrival.

I was very sorry and still frightened. It seemed as though fate was against me. On our way up, as my father was passing a place by the name of 'Bad Rock', many big boulders started rolling down, forming an avalanche blocking our path. It was two hours before we could continue our journey.

We reached home without further incident, and I was very glad when my mother gave me a hot bath, a cup of coffee and put me to bed as though I were a baby. I was very glad to go to bed to shut out all those horrific thoughts.

Thirteen-year-old girl

I was at home when I turned on the radio, to hear the news. The news I got was very shocking, it was a hurricane warning. We were told to buy special amounts of food and other necessities. The news was broadcasted at two p.m. and two hours later it started.

By now everyone was at home. Shops, stores and other business places were closed, and everyone waited this dreadful happening.

The seas started making a horrible noise, while the waves rolled angrily and devouringly. I looked out of the window and saw the winds tossing the trees here and there with violent force. The roofs of the houses were lifted and thrown into the yards of other houses.

People were crying and praying because more and more the water was rushing in and out of their homes, to get refuge with others that had not as yet been destroyed.

To keep the coldness from us we lit a huge fire and sat around it, eating some delicious hot porridge. While eating, we heard a loud crashing noise, and when we looked, we saw that a coconut tree had fallen onto the roof of our house, causing the wind and rain to come in more freely and desperately.

About half-past five the wind grew so much stronger that we began to tremble and murmur with fright and longing.

At six p.m. the hurricane ended abruptly and everyone was glad. We slept very soundly through the night, and in the morning the sun was shining brightly, the birds were singing sweetly and everything was normal and usual.

After clearing up, we prayed, that nothing like that will ever happen to us again.

Thirteen-year-old girl

On September the thirtieth 1963, I had the most memorable experience of my life. This is a live story of how it all happened.

On the beautiful morning of September the thirtieth, I, because of illness (influenza), stayed away from school. The morning was bright and sunny, but slightly windy. My three brothers had actually gone to school, so Vernon, a cousin of mine, my younger sister Linda, my mother and I were at home.

All of a sudden the wind began increasing and so I began to question my mother, 'Mammy, did storm ever come in Tobago?' I asked. 'Yesson, once when you was a little baby,' she said. 'But Mammy, look like a storm, look how the banana trees falling down,' I said. 'Boy don't talk stupidness, eh.' But the wind continued increasing. Then I heard Mammy's voice saying 'Boy it look as though yuh talking truth, yes. We better go upstairs.'

By the time we were upstairs and finished closing the windows, there was a resounding crash. The avocado tree, laden with beautiful fruit had fallen about two yards from the northern side of the house.

Coconut trees all around the house kept falling, some of their heads twisted as though the mighty hand of some unseen giant kept wringing them. Limbs of the cedar and bayleaf tree were being hurled like arrows through the air. There was a deathly calm.

At about one p.m. the first part of the hurricane had passed, and the principal of the elementary school urged all students to try to get home before the second half struck. Fortunately my elder brother reached home in time.

Vernon and I, at the interval of the hurricane, went out to the back yard to gather coconuts (water nuts) for drinking purposes when the second half came.

The second half of the hurricane came from the southeast just opposite to the first part; it came with a terrific force and a spinning motion, at about 120 m.p.h. The noise the wind made was like that of a jet plane whistling through the air.

In front of our house there are two large cedars and a bayleaf tree. Had it not been for these trees our house would have been destroyed. Like a boy raising the roof of his toy house, half of the roof of the shop which is also in front of the house came flying through the air and smashed with unbelievable force against the cedars and bayleaf tree. It wraped neatly around the trees like the hand of a man around match sticks.

The wind continued blowing with sheets of rain splashing against the house. Just to say how strong the wind was, Vernon and I went downstairs. When we opened the door both of us together could not close it back because of the force of the wind.

The wind decreased slowly after its destroying work was finished.

Nine people died, four-fifths of the houses were either destroyed completely or damaged. At the end of the hurricane, the island looked as though bombs had been dropped ten feet apart all over the island.

Thirteen-year-old boy

The structures of these essays, following the gradual and portentous growth and explosion of the hurricane and the calm and aftermath of its destruction, are dramatic and tragic in themselves. There is a natural conflict and climax in the event itself, and also in the children's response to it that seemed ideal for a theatrical experience. If they could act out a situation caused by the hurricane, and transpose their stage into their island, it seemed that such a play would reflect very much their own world, and their knowledge of themselves up against the most violent upheaval in their lives. It would be an organic extension of their identities. The people in Trinidad and Tobago have a very strong dramatic tradition which has kept its popularity in the Carnival and 'Old Mas' ', but somewhere drama at this school had distanced itself from their lives and gone to Shakespeare. It had become a part of the inhibited, academic world of the G.C.E. syllabus and 'proper' English language and literature. Now it seemed very necessary to bring it home again, in a way that caused it to reflect real life and experience.

Using the structure, and much of the material of the essays that the children had written, I conceived the framework of a short play about the hurricane. I suggested themes and guidelines for individual speeches, hoping that the players would improvise themselves, and use their own speech rhythms and structures to go in their own directions and forge out their own dialogue from the guide-lines I had given. I was a foreign, white teacher, paid by the government to train the children towards their G.C.E. certificates and I was writing these speeches in received English. So to make their dramatic experience anything like authentic, the children would have to be both emotionally and verbally creative, and remember and imagine vividly the heavy experiences of six years earlier. Some of the cast hardly veered from the ideas and themes I had suggested in the guide-speeches, only saying them in a semi-dialectal way, and I wondered if I had imposed too much of a structure on them. But the actor playing the main character—Hawkins—and also those playing Mrs Daws and the fisherman Carrington, only used the suggestions in the guide-lines for bases of high flights of improvisation in the language they knew best. Some lines were already fixed—such as those spoken by the 'Spirit of the Hurricane', a morality play figure who speaks like a stranger in 'proper' received English—and a few stylized lines spoken while the hurricane is blowing in its fury, but new lines and movements were often bursting out at all moments in the more realistic sections of the dialogue. The character of 'Hawkins' came to life very much because of the huge creative charge given to the part by its actor. He lurched, sprawled, belched, poured buckets of water over himself, and really lived

the part, making it grow in his own style. Later on in the year
when he was reading the part of Bottom in the Shakespeare
text we were studying for 'O' level English literature, he read
using many of the traits he had developed as Hawkins. He
began to see Shakespeare inside the context of his own world.

We tried to suggest the elemental fury of the hurricane by
using the natural sounds that were available to us, in a discordant combination which reminded many of the audience of
the real cacophonous experience. The frantic banging of three
African drums out of time with one another combined with the
crashing of galvanized iron sheets beaten by pieces of lead pipe
accompanied the loud and terrified shouts and screams of
human voices. This was synchronized with the stylized cruel
and violent movements of figures at the front of the stage,
struggling with the monstrous wind. At the back of the stage,
various pieces of debris—palm branches, coconut husks, pieces
of wood, pipe, tree-trunks—were hurled from wing to wing.
And behind the action and sound the lighting went on and off
in intermittent and uneven flashes, lighting up the stage, then
plunging it again into darkness. The total effect became a
multi-media experience into which the children flung themselves
with a combination of remembered fright and passion, and
dramatic discipline. The sound stopped and started, leaving brief
periods of uneasy silence in which the characters said their
stylized lines, often punctuated by short, violent bursts on the
African drums and flashes of coloured lights. The use of folk-
songs at the beginning and end of the play suggested the same
continuity of life before and after the disaster that the children
had expressed in their own accounts of the hurricane. The play
was always a living and growing thing, and by the time they had
acted it publicly several times—each time adding fresh embel-
lishments—and won the nation's Junior Arts Festival with it,
it was really the children's play, a reconstruction of their own
experience.

We had tried to show the island as a real place: real in the
sense of being a place of real men who eat and fish and drink
and sleep and suffer. To make the stage a world for Tobago,
certainly, but also as part of a greater and bigger world, giving
it the poetry of reality, of children at ease with their own language, on their stage, their island, their world:[4]

It is not enough
to pray to Barclays bankers on the telephone
to Jesus Christ by short wave radio
to the United States marines by rattling your hip
bones.

I
must be given words to shape my name
to the syllables of trees

I
must be given words to refashion futures
like a healer's hand

I must be given words so that the bees
in my blood's buzzing brain of memory

will make flowers, will make flocks of birds,
will make sky, will make heaven,
the heaven open to the thunder-stone and the volcano
    and the unfolding land.

It is not
It is not
it is not enough
to be pause, to be hole
to be void, to be silent
to be semicolon, to be semicolony;

fling me the stone
that will confound the void
find me the rage
and I will raze the colony
fill me with words
and I will blind your God.

I Thought You Loved the Fishermen

Characters

Spirit of the Hurricane
Peter Hawkins (a fisherman)
James (his son)
Salome (his wife)
Rebecca (his daughter)
John (his nephew)
Lucy ⎫
Mary ⎭ (friends of Rebecca)
Mrs Daws (a woman from a neighbouring village)
Carrington (a fisherman)
Men and women of the village
Scene: A fishing beach in Tobago
Time: Early Monday morning, 30th September 1963

Prologue (played in front of the curtain)

The stage is bare, the curtain closed. From behind the curtain comes the sound of a group of voices singing:

1 Johnny Grotto was a fisherman son
   yea, yea, yea ma boy.
   Johnny Grotto was a fisherman son
   A long time ago.

2 He went out to sea to catch fishes for me
   yea, yea, yea ma boy.
   He went out to sea to catch fishes for me
   A long time ago.

3 The sea was so rough and the seine pulling tough,
   yea, yea, yea ma boy.
   The sea was so rough and the seine pulling tough,
   A long time ago.

4 He ketch plenty fish and he make a nice dish
   yea, yea, yea ma boy.
   He ketch plenty fish and he make a nice dish
   A long time ago.

(*As soon as the singing stops, two heads emerge from the middle
of the curtain. They take a long look, with a semicircular
movement of the head scanning the audience, then their figures
appear from behind the curtain. They are the* Spirit of the
Hurricane, *a bi-sexual, composite personality. The woman moves
with exaggerated feminine charm, the man with an arrogant
virility in his gait. She talks seductively, he talks blusteringly,
and with an inflated self-importance. They meet in the middle
of the stage.*)

Man	For a start, they got my name wrong.
Woman	Because I have no name.
Man	They called me Flora for convenience.
Woman	But that's excusable, There' something very feminine about me. I'm passionate and fierce, and men's dreams Are nothing to me, neither are their schemes.
Together	*I destroy them all.*
Man	They insult me when they give me only one name Or only one sex, for that matter.
Together	*For I am all, and Both. And my destruction knows no names, no categories. I only destroy, I am very uncomplicated.*
Man	Yes, I am a man too you know. I have his muscles and his deadly unconcern And remember, he has invented Far worse things than me. So as I am only an amateur I will not contest him.
Together	*I will only destroy him.*
Man	And then, Only if he gets in my way.
Together	So you see, I am not vicious, And he is of no real interest to me.

Woman   So, if I seem a little strange to you,
It is only because I am foreign,
And I haven't been a very frequent guest.

Man   But I think you will remember me,
For I have a somewhat noticeable personality.
Shall we say I leave an impressive card,
Which I made available to all of you.

Woman   Tobago, you ask, 'Who sent me?'
who despatched me here?

Man   Well, that is not for me to say.

Together   *But now I've come to watch this play,*
To make sure that it gives no clues.
For I am possessive of my secrets.
Give me a chair.

(*He and she both click their fingers, and improvised seats are brought on to both sides of the stage by grunting fishermen. They take up their seats on either side of the stage and remain there, scrutinizing the action, for the duration of the play.*)

Scene 1

The curtain opens. The lights suggest a gradual sunrise. The lighted stage shows Hawkins, *asleep in an apparent stupor, half in, half out of a small fishing boat, stage left. The setting is a beach, suggested by backcloth, nets, driftwood, palm branches, coconuts, sand and various items of flotsam. A rum bottle, empty of its contents, lies significantly beside* Hawkins. John *and* James *rush in, excited, bubbling.*

James   Papa, Papa, ooooh Gosh, Papa.

John   Mr Hawkins, Mr Hawkins, wake up Mr Hawkins.

James   Quick Papa, the fish, the fish. (*He prods and pokes* Hawkins *who grunts and snorts. Then both boys pull* Hawkins *from the boat and drag him downstage.*) Plenty fishes, plenty fishes, so many fishes.

Hawkins (*Waking sluggishly*) Wha' happen? Wha' happen? Wha' you doing? You madman boy? I' your father boy. You doesn't grab hold of my leg and pull me so.
(*He has a comatose expression, and makes unco-ordinated attempts to grab his son. He speaks with a certain slur*) Why you wake me like this? And me having a good sleep. Oooh God, your mother must have made a madman when she make you. Get out, get out, or I'll grab hold of you and cut all of you tail with blows. And you too young Webster, I see yo' father, I'll get he to beat you.

James Noooh, Papa. Me no sick in me head, I no madman. It's the fish, get your net. Look, look at the sea. See the pelicans. See they diving all the time. It have a hundred pelicans out there, all diving and eating. (*Points straight at the audience, in the place of the sea.*) Look how fast they dive, oooh God, so quickly boy. They flash and they dive and then they go back for more. I never see they dive so quickly and so often. The sea is calm, but the big-ben and they dive so much, that they making they own waves.

Hawkins Uuuhh?

John And Mr Hawkins, the fish, the little fish is jumping like the sea too small fo' them, as if they is being squashed out of the sea because they have no room. Oooh, Mr Hawkins they is jumping, they is jumping. It must have more fishes than water out there. Go and get yo' net Mr Hawkins.

Hawkins I never yet did cuss young children, but you are bad, bad, worse than men. Making joke to me when I is in this condition and I is sleeping good. I shall cuss you so hard, and beat you boy if you don't give me peace.

Boys	But Papa . . . Mr Hawkins . . . I not lying, not making joke . . . the fish, the fish.
Hawkins	Fish? Fish you say boy? (*He speaks ferociously, and the boys cower*) Boy, you has a hole in you head? You has a big space boy? You vacant there, eh, eh? Fish? You know boy, no fish here. De fish gone away and they not coming by here again this month. All day Friday, not fish boy, not a tail, not a sprat. None Saturday too. Wha' you trying to tell me boy? I get the man to look at you head. Oooh Lord, I breed a lunatic for a son who run about with a set of lunatic friends.
James	(*Indignant*) The big-ben were diving plenty yesterday, I saw them.
Hawkins	Boy, I get him to look at you eyes too. Boy, you knows that I don' fish on a Sunday. I let God stock up he fishpond. I is a God-fearing man, I don' fish no Sundays.

(*Enter* Salome *and* Rebecca. Salome *walks fiercely across the stage,* Rebecca *filters into the background.* Salome *is wild and contemptuous. She sees* Hawkins, *and stamps up to his prostrate form, glowering heavily*)

Salome	Well, look at you man, look at you. You have a good rest eh? (*very sarcastically*) a good sleep? You mattress nice and soft? You pillow keep your head nice? You like the beach better than your home eh? Better than me eh? I smell your tongue and you mouth from here man. I set fire and put match to you' breath. All of we go up bang. It blow up Tobago man, all of we get blasted away.
Hawkins	Okay, okay, okay. I cant get no peace in the place. My family 'sposed to look after me. Instead you make my life misery. You does tear me 'part.

Salome   You drink up rum all afternoon and all evening
           and all night, you lime all day and then sleep
           in drunk sleep on the beach until the morning.
           You 'sposed to be a fisherman, but you doesn't
           pitch boat. You doesn't mend net. You doesn't
           catch fish. You does only catch rum, then you
           does drink it. You does only drink like a
           fisherman. And now with all the pelicans diving,
           and yesterday the little fish was all jumping up
           like it was Carnival and they playing mas.

Hawkins It don't have no fish this month I tell you. De
           fish and them they gone away. And you know
           I doesn't fish on Sundays. I let God stock up
           he fishpond.

Salome   He fishpond, eh? He stock you up from his
           rum-pond more like.

Hawkins He will provide.

Salome   He provide you with rum. Why you always
           bringing God into it. Why you always insult he
           by making he defend you and what you do.
           Can you fish on a Sunday? He say 'NO' you
           say. Can you drink rum on a Sunday, all Sun-
           day evening to Monday morning? He say 'Yes'
           you say. Why you say that? Why you always
           bringing he down to you lazy level. Why you
           blame he, when you have the power to change
           you' lazy self. I so vex with you.

Hawkins (*Holding his head in desperation*) Woman, woman,
           you stop getting at me, you hear? As soon as
           the morning starts, you start too, and you does
           go on until the day ends. You want to know
           why I does drink rum? 'cause then I doesn't
           hear you so well.

Salome   You doesn't see so well either. You don't see the
           fish when they is jumping up in front of you,
           right up you' nose, saying you could get a good
           catch if you wasn't the laziest man in Tobago.

(*Enter* Mrs Daws *at a run. She is flustered and puffing.*)

Mrs Daws   Hawkins, man Hawkins.

Hawkins   Good morning Mrs Daws.

Mrs Daws   Hawkins man. Get out you' net.

Hawkins   You too Mrs Daws? I thought you was a friend of mine. De whol' world gone mad around me. No peace, no peace.

Mrs Daws   No man, I just come from round the rocks. (*She gropes towards the boat and sits down.*) They get a big, big catch in Grafton Bay. I seen they get whole of Black Rock up there pulling seine. Sixty, seventy, hundred people, right up the beach pulling that net. Net full, full with jacks. No big fish, only jacks. Is queer Hawkins. The sea and them so calm and yet the little fish all swimming in shoals. Hundreds, thousands, all come inside the bay. The water's thick, thick, solid with jacks.

James   (*Proudly*) Se Papa, you did not breed lunatic when you breed me. I right, I right.

John   (*Jumping up*) We right, we right.

Mrs Daws   I never seen nothing like this, and all those fishes, those little fishes. Everybody get bucket and boxes and tins and pans and thing and them all carrying them home. But Hawkins, I never seen nothing like those fishes. As they die, they is making a funny, scary squeaky noise, and their eyes popping right out of they sockets. And as they dying they shaking and quivering and they is almost saying something to you, as if they is warning you 'bout something and they is really pleased. Is weird, is strange man, Hawkins, I was scared studying them fish die.

Hawkins   (*Reassuringly*) Tha's not strange. The little fish,
          they does always act so. When they catch they
          head in the net they does strangle in the twine.
          Then they does choke like Hell, and they eyes
          come right out, and look like they going to open
          out and bite you all up.

Mrs Daws But they doesn't squeak like that man. They
          not 'customed to make no noise usually, nothing
          like that. Ther's millions of fishes out there, all
          making that choke, that grate. I tell you they
          trying to tell de fishermen something. They has
          a message, they all choking in different sound
          and pitch. You hear it all over the village.

Salome   (*Still aggressive*) You see what you missing by
          lying here drinking plenty rum? Get the net in
          the sea and catch me fish. You kids does need
          food, even if you can live on rum.

Hawkins   Oooh God, dey says it have no rest for the
          wicked. What I done eh? A good living man
          like myself? Boy, boy, get me bucket of water
          boy.

(*Exit* James *in a hurry*)
(Hawkins *staggers to his feet, looks towards the sea, rubs his
eyes and looks again*)

Hawkins   What? wha' happen? wha's going on? Ooooh
          God, look at the pelicans. I can't see no sky, no
          sea, no horizon only a set of birds in de place.
          There is fish out there you know. There must be
          some fish? what, de fish must be jumping from
          here to Trinidad? Is that rum I been drinking, is
          that rum. I seeing things. Is that rum. Boy, boy,
          is that rum I been drinking.

(*Enter* James, *who staggers across the stage with a bucket of
water.* Hawkins *pours water over himself and looks again*)

          What? They is still there.

Salome   You telling us news? You BBC? You Radio

Trinidad? You get transistor inside you' head?

Hawkins   Is a miracle I tell you. God has done a trick for us. That's because I keep his holy day and show respect see. You boy, get out the boat, and you Webster get the nets out. And don't distract me woman wid you talk. I have work to do.

(*Exit* Hawkins *with* Boys *in a hurry*)

Mrs Daws   Oooh Lord, the fish and them send everybody mad.

Salome   He always mad, he don't need no fish to be mad.

Mrs Daws   You see how the sea is so calm. You ever seen it like that?

Salome   No I not studying the sea, look up there. There is big clouds in the distance, and the calm will soon go, and so will the fish. So he better get he nets quick, if he can move with all that rum inside he.

Mrs Daws   Come, come I going to pull more seine, and make some grog for de fishermen. Oooh, the fish, the fish . . .

(*Exit* Salome *and* Mrs Daws *running*)
(*The stage darkens and slides into a grey, overcast gloom.*
Rebecca, *who has sat quietly at the back of the stage right through the scene, comes slowly forward, staring at the menacing sky on all sides. She shivers. She holds out her hand to find rain. Then she moves off the stage with anxiety and trepidation*)

Scene 2

Later that morning, same beach.
Enter Men and Women of the village. *They are pulling in a seine net, and move stylistically across the stage from left to right to the accompaniment of African drums, singing, 'Johnny tief all the money, Pull away me boy'.*
They exit. Then enter Rebecca *and her friends* Mary *and* Lucy. *They are carrying buckets and tins filled with jacks. They are very exhilarated.* Rebecca *moves upstage.*

Lucy   We pull and we pull Girl, but the net and them keep on snapping, but we caught plenty fishes you know.

Mary   Everybody who pull carry home at least five bucketfuls.

Lucy   But girl, why only the little ones? With all them jacks there should have been much bigger fishes. I don' understand. Not one redfish or carit or bonito or thing. The big fish should have been inside of the bay, having a big meal of the little fishes. Then we should have got them.

Mary   Oooh, what you mean Lucy? You hush yo' mouth. You complaining when we have got all these fishes? We have fishes for a week in one one catch, and you is ungrateful.

Lucy   (*indignantly*) Me no moaning, and me no ungrateful. Gul, I just curious, that's all. I don' understand. There is always big fish when the little ones is jumping, and yet they not here today. They must be out in the deeper water somewhere, or swimming under the rock. Why they not here then?

Rebecca   (*Coming forward to the front of the stage, in between* Lucy *and* Mary) I don't care why not. Girl I just grateful. You remember Sunday School yesterday? You remember the lesson? What the man say? How the fishermen, Peter and them, was fishing in the sea in Israel, and they was no fish? and they fish all day and still no fish? And then come Jesus and he say, 'what you men doing with no fish?' And Peter he say, 'the fish gone way sir, there no fish here today.' And so Jesus say to he, 'Put your nets over the other side of the boat.' So they do this, and Gul, they get lots, lots, plenty, plenty, fish like we today. You hear the teacher yesterday, he

say God loves the fisherman, like my Daddy.
He love we, he love we, and so he fill we net for
we.

Mary   Yes. And them fishermen in the bible din' catch
no carit or shark or any big fish you know girl.
They was all small like our fish, because Jesus
had to do miracle to make them feed the crowd.
And a little boy carry them in he bag. So they
was small girl.

Lucy   Why yo' stupid Mary? It don' have shark in
Israel. They only has little fish. We has much
bigger fish in Tobago.

(*Exit* Lucy)

Rebecca   (*Looking to the sky, and putting out her hand*) You
feel rain? I think I felt a few spots Girl. Look out
to sea, and up there over the fort. The sky is
dark Girl, and behind them clouds is even
blacker.

Mary   (*Happily, as they wander off stage*) No matter, we
get enough. It can rain and blow for weeks if it
want.

(*Exit* Mary *and* Rebecca, *downstage left. As they move off enter*
Hawkins *and* Carrington, *both slightly drunk, leaning on each
other. They sing 'Rum Glorious Rum, when I call you you
bound to come'*)

Hawkins   What you think about all this Carrie? All them
jacks, and them so contorted and scared and
choking. They not 'customed to die so, you know.

Carrington   Well Mr Hawkins, me no question this. Everything come to he who wait. We done we waiting
all last week, and now is time for them to come
to we. Is not before time Mr Hawkins, we been
good, patient man, and now is we due. It don't
have nothing strange, nothing sinister Mr
Hawkins, we been good, patient christian men.

(*He opens a rum bottle that he holds in his hand*)
You like a little drink, a little swig? I think we
found good reason to spread joy. I never caught
so many jacks before.

Hawkins   (*with an affected reluctance*) Yes sir, I will take
a drop, although is bad for me during the week.
I don't normally touch it during the week. You
know that Carrie.

Carrington   Yes of course, yes of course man. You is a Satur-
day man, and then you is wild.

Hawkins   (*His ego flattered*) Well, I hope I is a man, flesh
and blood Carrie, and I has my little weakness
and indulgences in moderation, of course, Carrie.

Carrington   (*Humouring him*) Of course, yes of course. You
is right. That's the word Mr Hawkins, *Moderation*.
You have another swig Mr Hawkins, as a
celebration of course, Mr Hawkins.

Hawkins   As a celebration, as an occasion Carrie, I will
take one. I always say the bounds of modera-
tion is always increased Carrie, when it have
occasion.

Carrington   True again Mr Hawkins. I always say an occasion make 'e own rule, otherwise it wouldn't
be an occasion.

Hawkins   (*Taking the rum as Carrington is drinking*) Right
again Carrie, right again. (*In the background
begins a slow throbbing beat of African drums,
quiet at first but gradually getting louder*) Carrie,
you is a wise man. You has no education, no
school education like me, because you never
went to Bishops. But you is a wise man.

Carrington   The winds is getting high Mr Hawkins. You
think we in for a storm? Is been hot last week.

Hawkins   Is good to have a purge now and then. Washes
we out a little. I calls it a purge Carrie, a purge.
Like someone pull on the chain on we and wash

we down. We is sinners all Carrie, and we need
to be washed out now and then. Is good for us.

Carrington   That is right Mr Hawkins, that is right. My ol'
man in Scarboro' he used to say that when the
rains wash we down and beat on the galvanize
like it were machine gun. He used to stand out
in the rain and make us do it too, and he say to
we, to my brother and my little sisters and me,
he say, 'Boys, and Victorine'—that's my little
sister, she gone up Charlotteville now, 'This is
good for you,' he say, 'you feel God direct,' he
say. 'This is good for you, it teach you humility.'

Hawkins   That's something we all need Carrie, that's
something we all need. (*Finishes the rum and
throws down the bottle; there is a loud burst of
drumming*) This is a high wind Carrie. It is a big
one. You see that cloud up there over the fort?
What she remind you of? (*The stage gradually
darkens*)

Carrington   (*Unconcerned*) Like a cloud, just a cloud man,
a very dark one, but just a cloud.

Hawkins   Look good man, look good. I mean the shape.
You got no power for seeing shapes Carrie. You
not an artist like me. You not got the imagination man, not like me. I see patterns everywhere.

Carrington   Is the rum Mr Hawkins. You seeing thing
because of the rum. That Bajan rum is good and
strong.

Hawkins   (*Annoyed*) I can take me liquor man, I can take
me rum. I don't see things that arn' there. You
know that Carrie. I is a good, hard drinker.

Carrington   Of course yes, Mr Hawkins of course.

Hawkins   (*Looking up to the sky*) I don' like that cloud,
and is creeping up. Is like a gundy Carrie, a big
crab gundy, and we is right between the

pinchers. (*He makes a significant gesture. By this time the stage has darkened over completely, and* Hawkins *and* Carrington *are mere silhouettes*) Is coming right towards us.

Carrington   You need some mo' rum man, we go and get another bottle.

Hawkins   Not now man, doesn't you study anything else? Them jacks is good and fresh. We go and have a cook.

Carrington   Yes, yes man.

Hawkins   But I don't like that crab gundy. Is ugly Carrie, very ugly. I think we in for a big storm. I worried for my little girl in we old house. (*He considers*) If de storm get really bad boy, I send my daughter into the church, she is going to be safe there boy, that's the safest place. Come on man we go and eat.

(*Crashing of drums suggesting the approaching hurricane*)

Scene 3

The hurricane in all its fury. The stage is empty. The lights flash on and off. Upstage various missiles are being hurled on the centre of the stage: from the wings come palm branches, coconuts, sheets of galvanize, piping, wood, buckets, etc. Accompanying this clatter is frantic, discordant drumming and screams and moans from the wings. Figures rush on from both sides of the stage in stylized attitudes of terror and fear. They fight against the wind and the noise and stagger and flounder around the stage, shouting 'My house, my house', or 'My child, my child' or 'The school, the school.' They exit. As the noise increases a Man and a Woman stagger on to the stage. As they shout the druming stops, but continues ferociously for five-second intervals between each line. They face the audience in horror, supporting each other. Stylized speech.

Man   The sea, the sea, it boils like broth, it knows no
           calm.

Woman   The trees and branches blow around my eyes,
           all roots are gone.

Man   See, see the sky. See the balls of woollen wind
           as they scream towards us.

Woman   Feel the frown of God.

Man   Hear the cries of men.

Woman   See their houses fly.

Man   And their children die.

Woman   Hear the animals screech.

Together As we all reach, reach, reach, reach towards you
           God.

(*Exit fighting against the wind, struggling to keep their feet.
More frantic drumming and hurling, with flashing lights. Enter
another* Woman *floundering on the stage. Between every phrase
she speaks is a short clip from the drums*)

2nd Woman The church! the church! The church is down. It
             smashed and it fell. Who was inside? Who was
             inside? I saw the wood break and the beams
             fall. Then the galvanize flew all around and cut
             the air and plunged into the church. I heard the
             crash and felt huge wounds. I felt my own flesh
             break and flow. Who was inside? Who was
             inside?

(*She exits. More cacophony. Then from the back of the stage
enter* Hawkins. *He is carrying the motionless* Rebecca *in his
arms, and he fights clownishly against the vortex. He is crying
in absolute grief and perplexity. He comes to the front centre of
the stage, lays down* Rebecca, *and kneels behind her*)

Hawkins Why? Why? It should have been the safest
           place. I told her to go there. I told her to go
           there. How could I know? What can I know?

What did she know? What did she think? Who
knows? Who thinks? O Jesus, Jesus, I thought
you was a friend of the fishermen. O God I
thought you loved the fishermen . . .

(Hawkins *picks up* Rebecca, *with the help of* Carrington *who
has emerged from the darkness at the back of the stage.* Hawkins
seems about to speak again. But at that moment the Spirit of
the Hurricane *rises suddenly from both sides of the stage, and
man figure places his hand over* Hawkins's *mouth, stopping
any more words, freezing the characters, and stopping all the
noise.* Hawkins *and* Carrington *carrying* Rebecca, *gradually
move backwards upstage and the curtain closes on them. The*
Spirit of the Hurricane *relaxes in front of the curtain.*)

Epilogue

Man	Well that really got quite earnest, didn't it?
Woman	But I won't say how warm.
Man	You know, sometimes I can feel quite guilty When I see what I do. And yet, like most of you, I only do a job. And after all, I would never blame you for that, So would you blame me?
Together	*Remember, I have no malice.* *So please don't think me too despicable.*
Woman	I know that we can never be friends, But that is no reason for us to be enemies.
Man	You see, I cannot help my own nature, neither can you yours, and I don't hate you. In fact, I must admit that sometimes . . .
Together	*I quite admire your heroism.*

Woman	So don't spoil things and embarrass me, by
	    asking, 'who sent me', 'who is my chief?' be-
	    cause awkward silences spoil any new relation-
	    ship.

Together	*And I can tell you nothing.*
Man	Don't ask me if I come from God
Woman	Or Satan
Man	Or Nature
Woman	Or Mohammed
Man	Or from the sins of man.
Together	Just know me and remember what I look like Remember my face.

(*They deliberately show their faces to the audience in histrionic gestures*)

Woman	Then, if I ever come again, then . . . Well, perhaps we can meet on a more cordial basis
Both	*Thank you for the chair.*
Man	By the way—Do I get a present for coming? Ha ha.
Woman	Well, perhaps next time—Ummmh?

(*In the background there is singing.* AZA BUIL' WA NEW BOAT)

Man	And please don't call me Flora. (*Indignant*) It really does sound a little too intimate, Almost if you liked me.
Woman	And I'm quite sure you don't feel *that* affection- ate Towards me.

(*Man raises his hand to his ear*)

Man	Well, listen to them now. Singing very nicely. They soon got over us, didn't they?
Woman	They will soon be happy again. It is amazing. I will never understand them.
Both	Well, sleep well. (*Pause*) I may not bother you.

Man Goodnight ladies.

Woman Goodnight gentlemen.

(*They exit behind the curtain, the singing goes on.*)

Concluding song:

1 Aza buil' wa new boat
Aza buil' wa new boat
Aza buil' wa new boat
An' 'e call am Tobago massa.

Chorus:

Goodbye Aza, Goodbye—O
Goodbye Aza, Goodbye—O
Goodbye O' mi baby,
An' 'e call am Tobago massa.

2 Aza ketch one big fish
Aza ketch one big fish
Aza ketch one big fish
An' 'e call am Tobago massa.

3 Aza cook one sweet pot,
Aza cook one sweet pot,
Aza cook one sweet pot,
An' 'e call am Tobago massa.

4 Aza take one big sleep,
Aza take one big sleep,
Aza take one big sleep,
An' 'e call am Tobago massa.

7

After awareness

there is no turning back from awareness.[1]
George Jackson

Awareness of the ideas in this account can only bring discomfort. There is nothing to feel satisfied in what the white man's words are doing to black people. But to merely raise children's consciousnesses to an awareness of alienation and discomfort is a futile and evil process, unless it is accompanied with some answers or commitment to alternatives. For George Jackson the awareness brought its torment and desperation:[2]

Why can't I rid myself of the sorrow and emotion that awareness has brought me? I get rid of the self-destructive force of error and ignorance only to be torn and miserable by what I discover.

It was only an active and complete revolt against his accepted identity given to him by his mother and his country that caused him to find love and discovery. He would not serve white words and images:[3]

For you there is only one standard of beauty, the Western standard. I revolt against this absurdity. I understand that this is all you have ever known, I allow for this, but you must be able to see by now that this model of perfection you have subscribed to in the past is no longer the fad. Black is black. I'm going to fulfil my role as a man, even if it kills me.

We know that this absurdity is not only the state of a black man living in a white man's world. We are all living in a society which divides us from each other, causes distrust, fear and loneliness. The black man's state is only one image of ourselves. We have poems, novels, plays that speak of a deep awareness of our absurdity and alienation, but where do we go from there? Having accepted his own particular image of absurdity, how does the black man act? How do any of us act?

There is a section in Mayhew's *London Labour and the London Poor*, published in 1851, where the author interviews a black beggar on the streets in Whitechapel.[4] 'Ladies give me halfpence oftener than men,' says the black man. 'The butchers call me Othello and ask me why I killed my wife.' And still today, the white man's commentary on the black man is often only a predictable cluster of clichés. Now if a West Indian immigrant, walking up the Mile End Road, should look up at the sign of the public house next to Stepney Green station, he will see 'The Black Boy'. He will see himself in a turban with a white feather, wearing a hanoverian flared coat, yellow stockings, lace cravat and cuffs, and black shoes with shining buckles. He will see himself with wheyed face, carrying a tray with a porcelain jug on it. He will see what the white man has done to his identity, and what he is still doing. The black man must take command of his own identity. He cannot trust the white man and his culture to organize and portray his life for him. Ways have to be found so the black child, whether he lives in the Caribbean, or whether he lives in Britain, can speak for himself and his own life without having to adopt white forms and values. He must grow up with his identity intact, unbetrayed. He must have control over his own personal and social growth. Jackson wrote to his mother:[5]

You have been failed, by history and events, and people over whom you had no control. Only after you understand this can you then go on to make the necessary alterations that will bring some purpose and value to your life; you must gain some control.

A dynamic movement towards more social control for black people in England has come in Bernard Coard's book for the

Caribbean Education and Community Workers' Association, *How the West Indian Child is made Educationally Sub-normal in the British School System.* Coard demonstrates how British white middle-class culture pressurizes the black immigrant child to hate his own blackness, refuse to admit it, and makes him rather see himself as white: 'the children are therefore made neurotic about their race and culture'. Everything in their social world speaks against their blackness:[6]

> The black child's true identity is denied daily in the classroom. In so far as he is given an identity, it is a false one . . .
> If every reference on T.V., radio, newspapers, reading books and story books in school shows 'black' as being horrible and ugly, and everything 'white' as being pure, clean and beautiful, then people begin to think this way on racial matters.

Coard tells his readers that 'pride and self-confidence' are what is needed by the black man faced with the pressures of white culture. He emphasizes the need for black community action, more parental control over education, black nursery schools and supplementary schools, Caribbean syllabuses, more West Indian teachers, investigations into IQ tests and streaming systems which favour whites, and an end to placing West Indian children in educationally sub-normal schools until they have had a minimum of two years in a normal school.

Black people living in white societies or societies afflicted by a legacy of colonialism are beginning to deal very radically with their cultural absurdity. They are making their insights known through their own presses and community newspapers. They know that the old domination and betrayal need to be completely removed. They are creating new directions, new beginnings:[7]

> What we have to create is a new man; a man who masters himself and his environment; a man who combines mental and physical labour and a man who in his daily actions can give free expression to his many and varied talents and capacities.

The awareness and recognition of themselves as prisoners of white culture and language is causing them to act in a stronger and more unified way to free themselves. This becomes everyone's struggle. It is a forerunner of any movement by any people under cultural and political domination towards social health and control over their own lives:

> All living in one community
> Thinking for each other
> Helping each other
> No betrayals.[8]

References

Introduction

1 Derek Walcott, 'Laventville', *The Castaway*, Cape, 1965, p. 33.
2 Frantz Fanon, *Black Skin White Masks*, Paladin, 1970, pp. 61, 165.
3 *Childhood and Society*, Penguin, 1965, p. 241.
4 Ralph Ellison, quoted in John Dixon's *Growth through English*, Oxford University Press, 1967, p. 19.
5 Fanon, op. cit., p. 27.

Chapter 1   Monostatus

1 Frantz Fanon, *Black Skin White Masks*, Paladin, 1970, pp. 38, 14, 16, 12, 26.
2 Ibid., p. 99.
3 *Journal of Black Poetry (winter-spring 1970)*, ed. Askia Muhammed Touré, vol. 1, no. 13, p. 100.
4 *Soledad Brother*, Penguin, 1971, pp. 61, 62, 97, 112.
5 Fanon, op. cit., p. 165.

Chapter 2   The island theme

1 Cheryl Fraser, 'Self portrait', *Children as Writers*, Daily Mirror Press, p. 42.
2 P. B. Shelley, 'Lines Written among the Euganean Hills', *Selected Poems* (ed. E. Blunden), Collins, 1954, p. 151.
3 Derek Townsend, *Caribbean Guide*, Allen & Unwin, 1970, p. 47.
4 Lord Kitchener, 'Ode to Tobago', *King of the Road*, Tropico Records, Port of Spain, 1969.
5 J. M. Cohen (ed.), *The Four Voyages of Christopher Columbus*, Penguin, 1969, p. 221.

Chapter 3   Language and identity

1 Penguin, 1969, p. 182.
2 *The Politics of Experience*, Penguin, 1969, p. 53.
3 'Codicil', *The Castaway*, Cape, 1965, p. 61.
4 B. Bernstein and D. Henderson, 'Social Class Differences in the Relevance of Language to Socialisation,' *Sociology*, *3*, 1.
5 *West Indian Children in London*, Bell, 1967, p. 31.
6 *The Times Educational Supplement*, 20 March 1970, p. 20.
7 Frantz Fanon, *The Wretched of the Earth*, New York, Grove Press, 1968, p. 314.
8 Edward Brathwaite, 'Caliban', *Islands*, Oxford University Press, 1969, p. 35.
9 *The Tempest*, Act I, Scene 2.
10 Act I, Scene 5.
11 *The Winter's Tale*, Act IV, Scene 3.
12 *Othello*, Act I, Scene 1.

Chapter 4   English against identity

1 Stanley Hewitt (ed.), *This Day and Age*, Arnold, 1960, p. 49.
2 Kenneth Ramchand (ed.), *West Indian Narrative*, Nelson, 1966, p. 102.
3 Ibid., Introduction, p. 10.
4 Ibid., p. 2.
5 Collins, 1963, p. 469.
6 Ibid., p. 209.
7 Penguin, 1966, p. 60.
8 Derek Walcott, 'November Sun', *The Castaway*, Cape, 1965, p. 45.
9 Stanley Hewitt (ed.), *This Day and Age*, Arnold, 1960, p. 60.
10 Aimé Césaire (trs. J. Berger and A. Bostock), *Return to My Native Land*, Penguin, 1965, p. 63.

Chapter 5   English for identity?

1 Edward Brathwaite, 'Epilogue', *Rights of Passage*, Oxford University Press, 1967, p. 86.
2 Michael Joseph, 1963, p. 36.
3 From Jonathan Kozol, *Death At An Early Age*, Penguin, 1968, p. 189.

4 Trinidad and Tobago Arts Festival Association, *Arts Festival Syllabus*, 1969, p. 17.
5 Ibid., p. 28.
6 Government of Trinidad and Tobago, *Draft Plan for Educational Development in Trinidad and Tobago, 1968–1983*, Port of Spain, Government Printery, 1968, p. 35.
7 Op. cit., p. 78.
8 Ibid., p. 33.
9 Jean Rhys, *Voyage in the Dark*, Penguin, 1969, p. 7.
10 V. S. Naipaul, *An Area of Darkness*, Penguin, 1968, p. 27.
11 Penguin, 1969, p. 207.
12 Penguin, 1969, p. 75.
13 Kenneth Ramchand (ed.), *West Indian Narrative*, Nelson, 1966, p. 1.
14 Edward Brathwaite, 'Legba', *Islands*, Oxford University Press, 1969, p. 15.
15 *The Merchant of Venice*, Act II, Scene 1.
16 Coleridge, *The Ancient Mariner*.

Chapter 6 Drama and identity

1 Frantz Fanon, *Black Skin White Masks*, Paladin, 1970, p. 158.
2 Frantz Fanon, *The Wretched of the Earth*, New York, Grove Press, 1968, p. 315.
3 Edward Brathwaite, 'Wake', *Islands*, Oxford University Press, 1969, p. 55.
4 Edward Brathwaite, 'Negus', *Islands*, pp. 66–7.

Chapter 7 After awareness

1 *Soledad Brother*, Penguin, 1971, p. 139.
2 Ibid., p. 84.
3 Ibid., p. 165.
4 Peter Quennell (ed.), *Mayhew's Characters*, Spring Books, 1950, p. 391.
5 *Soledad Brother*, p. 67.
6 New Beacon Books, 1971, pp. 30, 28, 29, 39.
7 *New Beginning*, vol. 1, no. 5, San Fernando, Trinidad, 2 April 1971.
8 Maxine McCarthy, 'Racial Harmony' in *Stepney Words Number 2*, Reality Press, 1971, p. 7.